Introductory Agility Workbook

by Clean Run Productions

An Eight-Week Training Program for Introducing Dogs to Agility

Clean Run Productions
35 Walnut Street, Turners Falls, MA 01376

Introductory Agility Workbook

Third Printing

Copyright © 1996, 1997, 1998 by Clean Run Productions

Published by   **Clean Run Productions**
35 Walnut Street
Turners Falls, MA 01376-2317
413/863-8303

Acquiring Editor and Chief Writer   Bud Houston
Editors   Linda Mecklenburg and Monica Percival
Contributors   Linda Mecklenburg, Monica Percival
Book and Cover Design   Monica Percival
Cover Artwork   Nancy Krouse-Culley, Bud Houston, and Valerie Pietraszewska
Book Illustrations   Jaci Cotton, Karen Gaydos, Nancy Krouse-Culley, Bud Houston, Jo Ann Mather, Pascal Peng, and Valerie Pietraszewska
Printing   Hadley Printing Company

ISBN 0-9653994-0-0

Contents

Program Director's Notes

This workbook represents an eight-week introduction to the sport of dog agility. The exercises and discussions here are intended for the instructors of an introductory program. Pages are included that are suitable for handout material for the students in the program.

This is a good time to call attention to the important fact that your students are human and not canine. Many of your students will be novices to the sport of agility and to dog training in general. For these students, you are providing a context for learning and forging the bond between canine and human athletes. You will be teaching the human how to communicate with his dog and how to cultivate the dog's learning attention. Some of your students will be experienced in training a dog for agility. For these students, you will provide a structure for introducing a new dog to the sport.

About the Logistics of an Introductory Program

While the presentation in this workbook may appear to suggest or endorse the one right way to conduct an introductory program, training programs for dog agility take a variety of forms. Programs differ in terms of basic training techniques, administration, length of program, and guidelines for admittance and graduation.

Guidelines for Admittance

The guidelines that you establish for admittance to your training program depend largely on your own philosophy for the program. If you are running a commercial training business you might hold to higher standards and insist, for instance, that dogs have taken an obedience class. On the other hand, if your training program consists of a group of friends getting together to introduce the family dog to agility or a small agility club that's trying to build support in the area, you might relax your standards. On page 129, you'll find a Dog Profile Form that is used by the New England Agility Team (NEAT) to get a clear picture of prospective agility students and their dogs. You may want to adapt the Dog Profile to your own use.

The bare bones guidelines for admittance should include:

- **Pre-payment of the training fee.** Be sure you have a clearly stated policy regarding refunds (if any) for cancellation. Many programs offer no refunds; others offer credit towards a future class.

- **The dog demonstrates attention to his handler.** This should be determined as a pre-assessment. If the dog has an AKC® title such as the CGC (Canine Good Citizen) or CD (Companion Dog), you can be fairly assured that the dog is enough under control to begin agility training. If the dog has no such title to citizenship or companionship, it might behoove you to conduct your own assessment of the handler's ability to control the dog.

- **The animal is in good health.** Many training programs require proof that a dog is current in its vaccinations. You could carry this a step further and require a dog to get a health clearance from the family vet before being admitted to your program. You do not want dogs that are severely dysplastic or blind (or possibly even deaf) in your classes. Agility might do these dogs more harm than good. Again, it might be a good measure to do your own pre-assessment. If a dog is terribly overweight, you would do the owner a favor if you advised him to get the dog into good condition before starting agility classes.

- **The dog is old enough for your program.** The training plan described here is not a puppy program. The editors of this workbook recommend that the dog be at least one year old before starting an agility program. Even at one year, not all dogs should be jumping their regulation jump height. You should carefully consider your policies in these matters.

Guidelines for Graduation

Do you ask for a *specific* degree of proficiency for a dog to advance beyond your introductory program? It's up to you. Your goal may be to just give the dogs a solid introduction to agility and push only as fast as the individual dogs are ready to go. However, if you do set criteria for advancement, you must apply the same criteria to *all* of your students. Otherwise you will foster hurt feelings. Failing a dog—and let's face it, that's what you are doing when you tell the handler that he and his dog cannot advance—does not really encourage the fragile human ego to continue with the sport. Your program will be more successful if you encourage and nurture your students.

At the very least, your guidelines for graduation should require the dog to attend at least six of the eight classes. This should be made clear in the registration material for the class. If the handler's schedule doesn't permit the kind of attention required to properly introduce the dog to the agility equipment, then the dog should be required to take the class again when the handler's schedule is more settled.

If you want to set up more specific standards for advancement, here are several you might consider:

- The dog must be comfortable on the obstacles with the handler working on either the left or right.

- The dog must be able to enter the weave pole chute as well as a tunnel from any angle.

- The dog must be under verbal control but may still be working on a leash or tab.

One training program in California requires that the handler construct or purchase a set of six weave poles and several jumps to practice with at home before graduating into the intermediate class.

What Your Students Should Bring to Class

When you confirm a dog's enrollment in your training program, use the opportunity to tell your new students what they should bring to class the first night. Here's a good list for you to work with:

- A buckle collar or a quick release collar. Choke collars and pinch collars should not be allowed.

- A 4" or 6" tab lead.

- A 6' obedience lead.

- Lots of the dog's favorite food treats. Some people don't really know what their dog's favorite treat is. They've been doling out Milkbones™ and Fido eats them, so therefore they must be his favorite treat. If you assess that a dog isn't particularly interested in the food motivator selected by his handler, you may want to suggest that the handler bring a *special* treat such as string cheese, Rollover™, Oinkeroll™, microwaved hotdogs, liver, etc.

- A toy motivator (such as a ball, a Frisbee™, or a squeaky toy).

- Water and a bowl for the dog.

- A hungry dog! For an evening agility class, recommend that your students delay the dog's dinner until after class. For classes earlier in the day, they should skip the dog's morning feeding. This tactic will make the dog's attention that much keener!

NOTE: Along with their confirmation notice, send each student the list of agility commands and the tips printed at the end of this section.

How to Divide Your Classes

Each class session in this workbook has three or four working "sets". A set is the collection of equipment for which one instructor is responsible during the class. It is usually better, though certainly not required, for one instructor to remain with the same set of equipment throughout the class. The students, divided into groups, rotate from set to set during the class. Divide your class evenly—one group of students for each set.

The sets are intended to be worked simultaneously by a large class or consecutively by a small class. If you are working sets simultaneously, it's necessary to divide your students into logical groups. The best way to divide a class is by jump height. This allows dogs of the same jump height to work together so that not a lot of time is spent adjusting bars. Of course, in a beginner's program you never raise the jumps very high so there isn't as great a division as at more advanced levels.

NOTE: Throughout this workbook we make reference to "big dogs" and "little dogs". In general, any dog that measures 16" or less at the shoulders is considered a little dog. Any dog measuring more than 16" is a big dog.

Another way to divide a class is by skill level. For example, if you use the data on the Progress Worksheets in this book to group together the dogs having difficulty with certain obstacles, it will be possible to fashion a remedial program for just those dogs. Dogs that are advancing more quickly can be given a more advanced program.

If you divide your class into several groups, the time that students spend on each set should be carefully monitored; otherwise, it's possible that there won't be enough time to get to all of the required sets. To make this work, one of your instructors must be assigned the task of keeping time. If there are four sets and four groups of students, for example, an hour should be divided into 15-minute working periods. The timekeeper will give a two-minute warning *prior* to each switch between sets and will announce clearly at the end of the 15 minutes that it is time to switch.

Setting Up for Class

From day one, be an advocate for teaching your students the proper work ethic for participation in this sport. Setting up equipment is a lot of work. Get your students involved. If you get them used to the idea that you're going to do everything for them, they will soon come to expect you to continue to do so. Get them used to doing a share of the work and they will always expect to do their fair share.

One possibility is to require half of the class to come 30 minutes early to help move and set up the equipment. Require the other half of the class to stay late to put equipment away and clean up the training site. Be prepared to get tough with students who won't do their fair share of work. Make them sit out a week if they don't help with the work!

Cleaning Up After the Dogs

Encourage your students to exercise their dogs before coming to class. However, accidents are sometimes unavoidable. Your policy should be that the handler is responsible for immediately cleaning up after his dog.

Some programs require that students always be prepared for such an accident by carrying at least one plastic baggie in a pocket at all times. This ensures that the mess is quickly cleaned up and that it's not "lost" or stepped in while the handler is searching the training site for cleaning implements.

Not Allowed!

By policy, you should not allow:

- **Aggressive dogs.** Dogs should not exhibit aggressiveness either towards other dogs or towards people.

- **Harsh training methods.**

- **Choke chains and pinch collars.**

- **Bitches in season.** Some clubs do not allow bitches in heat. Other clubs can function adequately if the bitch is diapered. You'll have to make the call.

- **Barking dogs.** Of course, all dogs bark. What you are guarding against here is the dog that barks without pause or purpose. This restriction is intended to placate neighbors that would be disturbed by a constantly barking animal as well as to make sure that instructors aren't struggling to be heard over the noise.

- **Dogs that run away.** If you can't catch 'em, you can't train 'em.

Don't Forget Your Instructors

Being an instructor is sometimes a thankless job. Often instructors train other people's dogs at the expense of training their own. We advocate a policy that sets aside time and facilities for instructors to put their own dogs on the equipment. In an ideal world, your instructors should receive financial compensation for sharing their expertise and expending time and effort in support of your training program. An unpaid instructor can soon become an unhappy instructor.

How to Use This Workbook

This workbook includes pages that are designed for you to copy and distribute to your instructors and your students. For each week of the program, you will find student and instructor handouts, Progress Worksheets, and Facility Layouts that you can copy. The following sections explain how to best use each of these tools.

We've put all the dense and tedious stuff in a technical appendix. Each instructor should read this material and become acquainted with the training philosophies described there.

Handouts

This workbook is designed so that pages can be copied as handouts. Handouts come in two forms:

- **Student Handouts**—Prior to your first class, perhaps along with the registration confirmation and other materials you send to new students, send them a copy of "Commands Used in Agility" and "Tips for the Thoughtful and Intrepid" which you will find on pages 11 and 12.

  Each week have ready for your students the pages labeled "Student Notes". Remember that your students will be avidly interested in anything they can get their hands on to read about this exciting new sport.

- **Instructor Handouts**—For each week of class, each instructor should receive the "Instructor Notes" with the Progress Worksheet for that week copied on the second side. Each instructor should also receive a copy of the exercise(s) for which he'll be responsible that week. Ideally, the instructors should receive their copies *at least* a week ahead of the scheduled class so they can mentally prepare for what they must do with their students.

  Instructors should also get a copy of the Facility Layout for that week so they can direct the work in setting up the equipment for that lesson.

  Encourage your instructors to make notes about what works *and* what doesn't work in the training program. Your program will improve by the empirical knowledge they earn while conducting classes. An instructor will develop a keener eye for training and performance issues by keeping copious notes on the process.

Progress Worksheets

On the back of each week's Instructor Notes is a worksheet—or if you prefer, a model for a worksheet—that is used to take attendance and track obstacle performance problems. Each week write the names of your students in the left column, along with their dogs' names. This will help you and the other instructors learn all of the new names you need to learn. It will also help you track attendance over the course of the program.

If a dog has a major problem with a piece of equipment, tell your instructors to put an "X" in the square aligning with the dog's name and the obstacle that the dog is having a problem with. On the following week's Progress Worksheet, you should use a colored hi-liter marker to indicate that the dog had trouble with the obstacle in the previous week's class. This will assist your instructors in setting the difficulty of the exercises for that day and in determining whether a dog should be allowed off-lead for exercises.

Facility Layouts and Facility Layout Worksheets

The Facility Layout is a design for placement of the obstacles on your training field. Some thought has been given to ideal placement of the obstacles in the field, considering how dogs will move through each exercise and how dogs and their handlers might line up or queue at the start of each set.

In the ideal world, we all have two acres in which to set up our training sets. In the real world, however, many clubs do their training in limited spaces. It's conceivable that there won't be enough space to set up all exercises for a given week at the same time. If your agility area is smaller than the ideal field, you must design the facility layout for each week *prior* to class. For this reason, blank Facility Layout Worksheets have been provided. Feel free to make additional copies for your use.

Designing the facility layout is no small task, you will find. You have to be very thoughtful about how the obstacles are going to be set up. There should be enough room between the sets so that dogs are not running into each other. This will be especially important when dogs are working off-lead. Consider too that only one dog will be working on a set at a time. You must leave room for dogs and their handlers to wait in line, and you must leave room for some kind of path for a dog finishing an exercise to get back to the end of the line.

Acknowledgments

We thank all of the people who have made contributions to this *Introductory Agility Workbook*. A special thanks to Linda Mecklenburg and Monica Percival whose beginning obstacle training methodologies are reflected in the philosophy of this book. We also want to say thanks to a wonderful corps of artists who have allowed us to use their work to brighten up these pages: Jaci Cotton, Karen Gaydos, Jo Ann Mather, Nancy Krouse-Culley, Pascal Peng, and Valerie Pietraszewska.

Obstacle Curriculum

	Jumps	Contacts	Poles/Table	Tunnels
Week 1	Introduce non-winged bar jump. Use two crossed bars—one end in 6" cup and one end on ground.	Introduce ladder. Introduce dogwalk elevated to 2' or 3'.	Introduce weave poles. Lean poles alternately left and right. Begin with poles flat on ground and then raise tips to 12" off ground.	Introduce pipe tunnel. Use either a barrel or the pipe tunnel compressed to 3'.
Week 2	Review bar jump. Wing on one side and non-winged standard on the other. Little dogs 6"; big dogs 12". Introduce tire jump with tire resting on ground.	Review ladder. Review dogwalk at 3'.	Review weave poles with poles leaning so that tips are 12" off ground; gradually raise poles until they lean 45° off center. Introduce table at 6".	Review pipe tunnel. Start at 3' and work to full length. Begin bending one end into a curve. Introduce collapsed tunnel. Use only the barrel.
Week 3	Review bar jump. Non-winged jumps. Little dogs 6"; big dogs 12". Review tire. Little dogs tire on ground; big dogs 12".	Review ladder. Review dogwalk at 3'. Introduce A-frame elevated to 3' at apex.	Review weave poles with poles leaning 45° off center. Review table at 6".	Review curved pipe tunnel, graduating to "U" shape. Review collapsed tunnel. Add 3' chute and gradually lengthen.
Week 4	Review bar jump. Non-winged jumps. Little dogs 6"; big dogs 12". Review tire. Little dogs tire on ground; big dogs 12". Introduce long jump. Two planks, bar jump between.	Review dogwalk at 3'. Review A-frame at 3' and then raise to 4'.	Review weave poles with poles leaning 45° off center. Review table at 6".	Review pipe tunnel in "U" shape. Review collapsed tunnel with 4' chute.
Week 5	Review bar jump. Winged and non-winged jumps. Little dogs 6"; big dogs 12". Review tire. Little dogs tire on ground; big dogs 12". Review long jump. Little dogs: two planks, bar jump between, 20" spread; big dogs: three planks, two bar jumps between, 30" spread.	Review dogwalk at 3'. Review A-frame at 4'. Introduce see-saw with no plank motion.	Review weave poles with poles leaning 40° off center. Review table. Little dogs 6"; big dogs 12".	Review pipe tunnel in various configurations. Review collapsed tunnel with 8' chute.
Week 6	Review bar jump. Winged jumps. 6" for little dogs; 12" for big dogs. Review tire. Little dogs tire on ground; big dogs 12". Review long jump. Little dogs: two planks, 20"; big dogs: three planks, 30". Use bar jumps between planks.	Review dogwalk at 3'. Review A-frame at 4-1/2'. Review see-saw, gradually introducing plank movement.	Review weave poles with poles leaning 35° off center. Review table. Little dogs 6"; big dogs 12".	Review pipe tunnel in "U" shape. Review collapsed tunnel with 8' chute.
Week 7	Review bar jump. Winged and non-winged jumps. Little dogs 6"; big dogs 12". Review tire. Little dogs 6"; big dogs 12". Review long jump. Little dogs: two planks, 20"; big dogs: three planks, 30". Use bar jumps between planks.	Review dogwalk at 3'. Review A-frame at 4-1/2'. Review see-saw with dog beginning to initiate plank motion.	Review weave poles with poles leaning 35° off center. Review table. Little dogs 12"; big dogs 18".	Review pipe tunnel in "U" shape. Review collapsed tunnel with 12' chute.
Week 8	Review bar jump. Winged and non-winged jumps. Little dogs 6"; big dogs 12". Review tire. Little dogs 6"; big dogs 12". Review long jump. Little dogs: two planks, 20"; big dogs: three planks, 30". Use bar jumps between planks.	Review dogwalk at 3'. Review A-frame at 4-1/2'. Review see-saw starting dogs from the ground.	Review weave poles with poles leaning 30° off center. Review table. Little dogs 12"; big dogs 18".	Review pipe tunnel in "U" shape. Review collapsed tunnel with 12' chute.

Teaching Props

In training we often use special equipment, or props, to assist in the training process. These props can be especially useful when introducing a dog to an obstacle and when doing remedial training with a dog in a problem area. Some of the props worth acquiring for your program include those listed below.

Sawhorses

Sawhorses of different sizes (3', 4', 4-1/2', etc.) can be used for creating reduced-height contact equipment. A sawhorse placed under the A-frame, for example, will allow you to set the obstacle at a lower height than would be supported by the chain lengths on some A-frames.

Cement Blocks or Milk Crates

Cement blocks or milk crates are also useful for creating reduced-height contact equipment. For example, you can place a 12' plank on two cement blocks to get dogs used to traversing a bouncy middle plank as they may encounter on some dogwalks. Or, you can create a mini dogwalk by setting up three 8' planks on two cinder blocks so you have an ascending ramp, a middle plank, and a descending ramp.

See-Saw

An adjustable see-saw is ideal for an introductory program. You could attach a 12' plank to a piece of 2" i.d. PVC pipe or to a log, or you could buy a readily adjustable see-saw. An adjustable see-saw is available from Pipe Dreams (see the "Agility Resource Sheet" on page 131).

Ladder

This workbook makes extensive use of a ladder in early contact training. The ladder helps a dog get a feeling for where his feet are. A 10' or 12' ladder works well, or a specially designed ladder is available from Pipe Dreams.

Weave Pole Wires

A specially designed wire is used to connect weave poles to form a "channel" in and out of the poles, requiring the dog to make the proper entry and weave down the line of poles without missing any pole. These are difficult to make at home; however, a commercial weave pole wire is available from Amigos Enterprises (see the "Agility Resource Sheet" on page 131).

Leaning Poles

The leaning poles method used in this workbook can be a set of metal stakes over which you slip lengths of PVC. However, the drawbacks to pound-in-the-ground stakes are that it's time consuming to adjust them and they can only be used outside. A commercial set of leaning poles that adjust in seconds is available from Pipe Dreams.

Barrels

In early tunnel training, a paper, plastic, or metal barrel is a good substitute for a tunnel. You should make sure the barrel is clean and safe, with no sharp edges protruding. The barrel should also be washed thoroughly— barrels are often used to store detergents and other agents which might be irritating to the dogs. Car washes are often good sources of barrels and sometimes you'll see newspaper ads for used "juice barrels".

Long Jump

For little dogs, place a 6" jump between two long jump planks. For big dogs, use two 12" bar jumps shuffled between three planks. Throughout the basic program, you should present the long jump to dogs in this fashion. The bar jumps can be removed when the dogs graduate to an intermediate program.

Traffic Cones

Traffic cones can be useful—you can rest a jump bar on the top of two cones if you're running short of jumps; you can set cones on contact planks to keep people from unsupervised use of the equipment; or you can place one or more cones on each side of an up ramp to help the dogs "square up" their approach to a contact obstacle.

Demo Dog

It is often useful to have an experienced dog available to demonstrate the desired performance for the obstacles you are introducing. For the weave poles in particular, it is helpful for students to have a clear vision of what they're working towards. If a suitable demo dog is not available (you need a dog that isn't offended by being yanked out of a crate for a brief performance and then shoved back in!), consider showing a short video the first night of class.

Agility Commands

The command you use to direct your dog to perform an obstacle is entirely up to you. There is no requirement in agility competition that you favor one command over another. However, once you decide what commands you want to use, it is very important to be *consistent* with those commands. The following table summarizes the standard set of agility obstacles and suggests some commonly used commands for each.

Obstacle Commands

Bar Jumps	Hup, Jump, Over
Long Jump/Spread Jumps	Hup, Jump, Over, Big Jump
Tire Jump	Hup, Jump, Over, Tire, Hoop
Weave Poles	Poles, Weave, Doodah-doodah, Wiggle
Pipe Tunnel	Through, Tunnel, Get In
Collapsed Tunnel	Through, Tunnel, Get In, Chute, Swoosh
Table	Table, Hup, Get On, Box
A-Frame	Climb, Walk Up, Ramp, Scramble, Frame, A-Frame
Dogwalk	Climb, Walk Up, Ramp, Dogwalk
See-Saw	Climb, Walk Up, Ramp, See-Saw, Teeter

Control Commands

Come	*Come!* means for the dog to stop whatever it is doing and come directly to you. In obedience, a solid recall usually finishes with a sit in front of the handler awaiting the next instruction. This type of finish is not necessary, nor even desirable, on the agility field.
Down	*Down!* means for the dog to lie down—chest, elbows, and the rear should be on the ground.
Stay	*Stay!* means the dog should remain in place until released by the handler. In the strictest obedience context, *Stay!* also means to maintain the current pose—a sit or a down or a stand.
Wait	*Wait!* means for the dog to stop forward motion or hold itself back. The dog momentarily pauses, eagerly anticipating that it may resume the task at hand or continue on its current path when released by the handler. Whereas *Stay!* is used when you *leave* the dog in a particular position and want him to maintain that position, *Wait!* can be commanded while the dog is in *motion*—you could use it when the dog is ahead of you and you want him to "wait up".
Sit	*Sit!* means that the dog's rear should be on the ground and his front should be upright.
Okay	*Okay!* is a quiet release command. It is typically associated with releasing a dog from its position in the down-side yellow of a contact obstacle or from a stay on the table.
Easy	*Easy!* means slow down and exercise greater caution in performing the current task. This allows you better control of the dog when approaching and departing an obstacle. The dog should look to you for an indication of when it's all right to resume full speed again.

Directional Commands

Turn Back	*Turn Back!* means to reverse direction (a 180° turn).
Left	*Left!* means turn to the left—the dog's left, *not* yours!
Right	*Right!* means turn to the right—the dog's right, *not* yours!
Go	*Go!* means continue in the present direction, possibly away from the handler.
Get Out	*Get Out!* means move laterally out to the side of the handler.

Tips for the Thoughtful and Intrepid

✫ You most effectively communicate what it is you want your dog to do by moving in the direction of the obstacle, supported by a hand signal. Your dog keys more on visual clues than on verbal, especially in the beginning. Concentrate on giving your dog a strong hand signal, and lining up your body to face the obstacle to be performed. Be sure to give your hand signal with the hand closest to the dog.

✫ If it is at all possible, do not speak the name of the obstacle until your dog is pointed towards, and focused on, that obstacle. Your dog will tend to move in the direction that his nose is pointed. Your task will be to make your dog's nose point where it is that you want him to go.

✫ In agility, unlike some other dog sports, there's no penalty for giving a command more than once.

✫ Reduce the "noise" your dog must listen to when performing. For example, you don't need to use your dog's name before every command. In general, it is not necessary to blather at your dog. Keep your working conversation to a minimum, saying just enough to motivate and direct your dog.

✫ Consistency in what you do is key to a successful working relationship with your dog.

✫ It is better to be upbeat and enthusiastic with your dog than not. Your dog will be sensitive to you getting angry or flustered or frustrated during a training session. It is your job to keep the dog happy. When your dog piles into the car to go to agility class, you want to seem him excited and enthusiastic and knowing that he's getting ready to have the most fun in the whole world—and there should be no one in the world he'd rather do it with than you!

✫ When training for agility, you need to learn to be a bit silly with your dog. Your voice must be a sublimely happy voice. You need to whoop and holler and cavort. When your dog does anything right—*anything*— reward the performance with joyful celebration. If your dog does something wrong, all it really means is that the dog didn't get it. So you don't do anything—you don't chastise and you don't bark.

A NOTE FROM BUD FOR MEN ONLY: I know it could be embarrassing being out on the agility course dancing and whooping around and crooning to your dog in a falsetto voice—especially with all the women watching. Let 'em laugh. You know, the only reason they tolerate us in this sport is because we move the big equipment and we have trucks. *You* can get the last laugh at the USDAA®, AKC®, or NADAC finals! But to get there, you're going to have to lighten up and have some fun with your dog.

✫ Control commands and directional commands should be taught independently and not confused with agility obstacles or exercises. These commands are perfectly suitable for teaching the dog at home between excursions to agility class. Don't wait for someone to give you a framework for teaching either; most agility curricula do not address either control or directional commands.

✫ What you do at home each week is as important or more important than what you do in class each week. You should use opportunities at home to teach your dog obedience, to socialize your dog, and to train on agility obstacles. This means that much to the delight of your neighbors, you will most likely at some time have agility obstacles and toys in your yard—much like those neighbors will have swing sets and other toys for their children.

Week 1: Instructor Notes

This week you'll start a new group of students on a long journey. If they knew how many hours of training and patient exercise are required for mastery of this sport, they might have second thoughts were it not for the simple fact that agility is fun and completely gratifying.

You will be a profound influence on each of your students. You will forever more be their first instructor. Your every word and instruction, and your every example to them, will help shape and define what they become in this sport. You will have the satisfaction of knowing that you started them on this journey.

Your chief obligations on this day will be to provide a safe and non-threatening playground for the dogs *and* to communicate to your students effective methods of training, using positive motivation.

Artist: Nancy Krouse-Culley

	Jumps	Contacts	Poles/Table	Tunnels
Week 1	Introduce non-winged bar jump. Use two crossed bars—one end in 6" cup and one end on ground.	Introduce ladder. Introduce dogwalk elevated to 2' or 3'.	Introduce weave poles. Lean poles alternately left and right. Begin with poles flat on ground and then raise tips to 12" off ground.	Introduce pipe tunnel. Use either a barrel or the pipe tunnel compressed to 3'.

Organizational Notes

It's a good idea to start a new class with introductions all around. As your students introduce themselves, check them "present" in the attendance column on the Progress Worksheet (on the other side of this page). Don't forget to introduce yourself!

Remind all the instructors to mark the Progress Worksheet if any students have trouble with one of the obstacles they are responsible for introducing.

Start the training session by doing the control exercise on page 17 with the entire group. Then break into groups for the training sets, if you're going to work multiple sets simultaneously. The training sets for this week include:

1. Introduce weave poles

2. Introduce non-winged bar jump

3. Introduce dogwalk and ladder

4. Introduce pipe tunnel

Required Reading

The instructors should read:

- "Training the Dogwalk" on pages 108–112.

- "Training the Weave Poles" on pages 124–126.

- Exercises for Week 1 on pages 17–22.

Week 1: Progress Worksheet

Instructors: Date:

Handler and Dog	✓ Attendance	Dogwalk	A-Frame	See-Saw	Weave Poles	Pipe Tunnel	Collapsed Tunnel	Bar Jump	Long Jump	Tire Jump	Table

GENERAL NOTES:

Week 1: Facility Layout

One square = 10'

	Set 2 Jump				Set 4 Tunnel		
		Set 1 Weave Poles					
	Set 3 Dogwalk & Ladder						

Week 1: Facility Layout Worksheet

Design your Facility Layout using a 1" = 10' scale (standard agility template)

Week 1: Exercises

Start the class by doing the control exercise with everyone. Then break into smaller groups if you're going to work the training sets simultaneously.

Control Exercise

Start the session with an obedience exercise to call everyone's attention to the basic control commands. Many students will have done basic obedience with their dogs, but others may have no concept of simple skills like *Sit!* and *Stay!* and *Come!* If there is a control problem with particular dogs, this exercise will make it clear.

- Prepare for yourself several tennis balls and a squeaky toy.

- With dogs on-lead and in heel position, heel everyone through the obstacle course. Form a line and instruct the handler at the beginning of the line to weave a random course among the obstacles.

- Halt and *Sit!* the dogs. Have handlers leave their dogs, going to the end of the leash, and then turn back to face the dogs. Hold that position for about 30 seconds and instruct everyone to return to their dogs.

- Heel about again, stretching your students into a long line along one edge of the agility field. Halt and *Down!* the dogs. Have handlers leave their dogs, going to the end of the leash, and then turn back to face the dogs. Anyone who feels really confident can drop the leash and move as far away as they're comfortable.

- After a minute, recall the dogs—*Fluffy Come!*

- Again, put your class back into a line. *Down!* the dogs as before and have the handlers assume a position facing the dogs. This time hold that position for at least three minutes.

By the end of three minutes, the dogs that have pretty solid obedience control will still be in their downs. All other dogs will be otherwise engaged. Add a little challenge to the exercise by weaving your way through the line of dogs. Throw tennis balls this way and that, and palpate the squeaky toy as you walk among them. This is a good distraction test, though not really all that fair.

At the end of this exercise you might want to make a short speech about doing homework. The basic control commands (*Come! Sit! Down!* and *Stay!*) should be taught at home frequently and consistently.

Make a note on your Progress Worksheet for dogs having difficulty with control. You should *not* let dogs with control problems off-lead in this class without very close supervision.

Artist: Jaci Cotton

Set 1: Introduce Weave Poles

This is an illustration of a set of competition weave poles. Your training poles might not look this way at all. Computer Artist: Pascal Peng.

Your set uses a weave pole chute of no more than six poles set up in a leaning poles configuration—the first pole leans left, the second pole leans right, and so forth, down the line. The poles are leaned away from center until the ends lay flat on the ground.

It would be very useful for you to use an experienced dog—an impressive weaving dog, if possible—to demonstrate the desired performance of the weave poles. As you demonstrate the poles, it's helpful to give your students a brief overview of the overall process for training the weave poles (explaining how the prop weave poles work) and also to explain that dogs won't learn to weave over an eight-week introductory class—and probably not even in a subsequent intermediate class. In most cases, learning the weave poles will require some work at home.

Instructions

This exercise is performed on-lead.

1. With the dog on his left, have each handler walk the dog down the chute of poles. Allow the dog to walk down the middle of the base while the handler steps over the weave poles on the ground. For dogs that are afraid of the base, use a food treat or a toy to help focus the dog as the handler leads it through.

This illustration shows a set of leaning poles for training. Computer Artist: Pascal Peng.

2. Repeat step 1 one more time or until all the dogs are comfortable walking along the base.

3. Raise the tips of the weave poles until they are about 12" above the ground.

4. If an extra body is available, assign a spotter to hold the dogs at the entrance of the poles; otherwise the job is yours. One at a time, handlers give the spotter their leash. The spotter holds the dog behind the opening to the poles. *The handler* trots down the middle of the poles, turns around, shows the dog a treat, and calls the dog. The spotter should hold the leash directly above the dog's head to keep the dog moving straight through the poles and then drop the leash as the dog gets to his handler.

   NOTES: If a dog is slowing down in the poles, have the handler back up as the dog comes toward him. This encourages the dog to continue moving forward as he nears the end of the poles. Also, the spotter should not allow the dog to leap through the poles—use the leash to hold the dog to a trot.

5. Repeat step 4 until your time with this group is done.

End of exercise. Mark your worksheet for dogs having trouble with the poles.

Set 2: Introduce Bar Jump

This is an illustration of a competition jump complete with wings. Your training jump will not include wings in the beginning and the bars will be set very low. Computer Artist: Pascal Peng.

This is an illustration of a non-winged bar jump that is set with the bars crossed for training purposes. Computer Artist: Pascal Peng.

Your set consists of one non-winged bar jump. The bars should be crossed in the jump standards, with one end in the 6" cup and the other on the ground.

The goal is to teach the dog to go between the jump standards on the handler's signal.

- Demonstrate how to square up your body for performance of the jump. Don't turn sideways to the dog. Face the jump and move directly toward it. As the handler passes alongside the standard, the dog has no choice but to go over the jump.

- Demonstrate a clear hand signal, using the hand closest to the dog, and pushing towards the jump.

- Remind your students to have a food treat available. Coach them to use the treat immediately as the dog clears the hurdle. They should give the dog immediate and enthusiastic praise.

Instructions

This exercise is performed on-lead.

1. With the dog on his left, the handler trots the dog over the jump. Give praise and reward.

2. With the dog on his right, the handler trots the dog over the jump. Give praise and reward.

3. The handler leaves the dog (drape the lead over the bars), positions himself on the far side of the jump, and calls the dog over the jump. If the dog will not stay while the handler moves away, you or a spotter should hold the dog. Remind this handler to practice stays at home before the next class.

4. Repeat steps 1–3 until your time with this group is done.

End of exercise. Mark your worksheet for dogs having trouble with the jump.

ON A REFUSAL: The dog does not get the food treat. The handler should not chastise the dog or otherwise make an emotional correction. That won't motivate the dog to come out and play agility. Simply withhold the treat and the praise. The dog will ultimately figure out what behavior earns the treat and praise, and what behavior earns him nothing.

Often a dog will refuse a jump because he is frightened or unsure of himself. It is better with these dogs to be soothing and encouraging rather than forceful and demanding. Take the extra time to encourage the dog over the jump. The handler should get on the opposite side of the jump, with the dog's lead passed over the bars, and encourage the dog over. Remember that praise and a food treat should be immediate and enthusiastic. You can also have the handler try standing close to the jump with the dog on-lead and then toss a toy or a **food tube** over the jump to encourage the dog to go over the bars. (See page 49 for a description of a food tube and instructions on making one.)

Set 3: Introduce Dogwalk and Ladder

Your set consists of a ladder, laid flat on the ground, and the dogwalk elevated to 2' or 3'.

Ladder Instructions

The purpose of the ladder is to make the dog thoughtful of where he places his feet. Large dogs and younger dogs, especially, tend to be unaware of what their back feet are doing. Each handler walks his dog through the ladder (on-lead) two or three times. Make sure your students are leading their dogs through this exercise completely under control. No running!

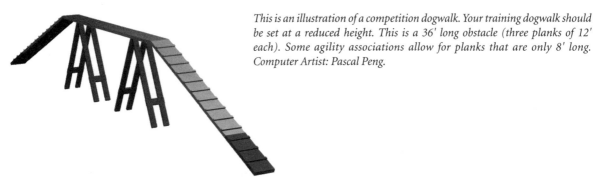

This is an illustration of a competition dogwalk. Your training dogwalk should be set at a reduced height. This is a 36' long obstacle (three planks of 12' each). Some agility associations allow for planks that are only 8' long. Computer Artist: Pascal Peng.

Dogwalk Instructions

These instructions are based on the twelve-phase training program, "Walking the Plank: The Dogwalk", which is included in its entirety on pages 108–112. The instructions below are a summary of Phase 1 and Phase 2 of the program. The dog should be wearing a buckle collar and a tab for this exercise.

1. Help each student lift his dog onto the *end of the down plank,* facing off the dogwalk. The handler should reward the dog with food and praise for remaining there. The dog can be in any position but standing is preferred. At first give the food directly to the dog; then place it on the end of the plank. The handler should signal to the food by pointing to it with the hand closest to the dog and touching it, encouraging the dog to focus downward to the end of the plank.

    NOTE: Some dogs are too large to pick up and put on the plank. In such a case, try positioning the dog alongside the end of the plank. Then, just swing the back end of the dog into the contact zone so the handler can at least reinforce the wait in the zone.

2. The dog is not permitted to leave the plank until the handler releases him with a quiet *Okay.* Handlers should not praise or feed the dog, or celebrate as the dog leaves the plank. You do not want the dog to associate leaving the plank with positive reinforcement—*positive reinforcement should occur only in the contact zone.*

    ON A REFUSAL: If the dog attempts to leave the plank, say nothing. Pick up the dog and put him back in the original position on the end of the plank. Reward the dog again for being in the contact zone. With some stubborn dogs, you may need to do this a few times. Do not get angry at the dog; just keep replacing the dog on the plank until he is willing to wait for a release command.

3. Repeat this exercise until the dogs are focusing on the end of the plank, anticipating the food reward, and waiting for release before leaving the plank. Do not continue to step 4 until you have achieved this! Dogs should advance as quickly as practical through the twelve phases of this program. However, they should advance only if they are being successful as described.

4. Place a food treat at the bottom of the down plank and then lift the dog onto the *center of the down plank.*

5. Command the dog to *Walk!* and then guide him forward. The handler should signal to the waiting food. The handler should not use a verbal command like *Wait!*—the dog is expected to stop at the end of the plank of his own volition. If the dog does so, he gets food. If he doesn't stop, pick up the dog and put him back on the end of the plank.

6. As before, the dog is not permitted to leave the plank until released with a quiet *Okay.*

End of exercise. Mark your worksheet for dogs having trouble with the dogwalk.

Set 4: Introduce Pipe Tunnel

Your set consists of the pipe tunnel compressed to 3'. To keep the tunnel bunched up, you'll have to secure it with bungie cords or tunnel holders. Alternatively, you can use a barrel with both ends cut out.

The goal is to teach the dog to get in the tunnel and go through.

- Explain to your students that the ultimate objective will be for your dog, when commanded to seek the tunnel, to get in and go through the obstacle from almost any angle or distance.

- Demonstrate for your students how to square your body up for performance of the tunnel. Don't turn sideways to the dog. Face the tunnel and move directly towards it.

- Demonstrate a clear hand signal, using the hand closest to the dog, and pushing towards the tunnel. Handlers should hold the lead in the opposite hand.

- Remind your students to have a food treat available. Coach them to use the treat and to give enthusiastic praise immediately as the dog exits the tunnel.

Instructions

This exercise is performed on-lead.

1. If an extra body is available, assign a spotter to hold the dog on-lead at the entrance of the tunnel; otherwise the job is yours. The handler goes to the opposite end of the tunnel and entices the dog through with a food treat or toy motivator. The person holding the dog should try to help keep the dog focused on the tunnel opening and his handler on the other side, but should not force the dog into the tunnel.

2. Repeat step 1 until the dog is happily diving through the tunnel.

3. With the dog on his left, the handler trots the dog towards the tunnel, releasing the leash as the dog enters. Give immediate praise and reward as the dog exits the tunnel.

4. With the dog on his right, the handler trots the dog towards the tunnel, releasing the leash as the dog enters. Give immediate praise and reward as the dog exits the tunnel.

5. Repeat steps 3 and 4 until your time with this group is done.

End of exercise. Mark your worksheet for dogs having trouble with the pipe tunnel.

ON A REFUSAL: The dog does not get the food treat. The handler should not chastise the dog or otherwise make an emotional correction. That will not motivate the dog to come out and play agility. Simply withhold the treat and the praise. The dog will ultimately figure out what behavior earns the treat and praise, and what behavior earns him nothing.

If the dog is really adamant in his desire not to enter the tunnel, he should *not* be forced. The handler of this dog needs to do some motivational homework in the time before the next class. The handler should take home a barrel or a tunnel for this homework. During the week, the dog's meals should be quartered and each portion used to lure the dog through the barrel or short tunnel. This is an extremely effective method of curing a dog of tunnel shyness.

This is an illustration of a competition pipe tunnel that is bent slightly into a "U" shape. To start with, your training tunnel will be straight and much shorter. Computer Artist: Pascal Peng.

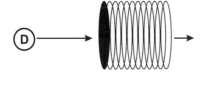

With the dog on his left (on-lead), the handler trots the dog towards the tunnel. The handler releases the lead as the dog enters the tunnel. Give immediate praise and reward as the dog exits.

Introductory Agility Workbook

Week 1: Student Notes

You have to learn to be a bit silly with your dog. Your voice must be a sublimely happy voice. You need to whoop and holler and cavort. When your dog does something right—*anything*—reward the performance with joyful celebration.

If your dog does wrong, all it really means is that the dog didn't get it. So you don't do anything— you don't chastise and you don't bark. Don't draw your arm back like you're going to hit your dog and never, never, never... hit your dog.

When your dog piles into the car to go to agility practice, you want to see him excited and happy and knowing that he's getting ready to have the most fun in the whole world—and there should be no one in the world he'd rather do it with than you.

Artist: Jo Ann Mather

Teaching Table Manners

Table manners are best taught at home. You don't really need a table. You need a reliable *Down!* for your dog; and in the case of AKC agility, you need both a reliable *Down!* and a reliable *Sit!*

Sit! and Down!

Train *Sit!* as follows. The first two or three times you command *Sit!*, immediately place the dog into a sit and reward. To place the dog in a sit, hold his collar with one hand. With your other hand, run your hand down the dog's spine and over his tail and then "tuck" his rear underneath him. This works much better than pushing straight down on the dog's rear since he will tend to resist you.

For the remainder of the training session, you will give the dog an opportunity to respond to your *Sit!* command before you follow through. However, if the dog doesn't immediately comply with the *Sit!* command, correct him by placing him into a sit. Then praise and reward. Always praise after a correction when the dog is doing what you want him to do.

Teach *Down!* while your dog is on-lead, positioned in front of you. Use a hand signal—an upraised arm with the palm flat and facing towards the dog—in conjunction with the voice command. If the dog doesn't immediately go down, your flat hand comes down on the dog's lead and forces him to the ground where you reward him. Your dog quickly learns to associate the upraised palm with your desire for him to assume the down position.

Once your dog is reliably doing a down, you can start moving further away from the dog and asking him to maintain the down for longer periods of time. Try standing 6' or 10' away while your dog is on his down. The dog should not break from the down position until you release him. If you have problems, put the dog on-lead and decrease the distance.

Training Tips

When first teaching *Sit!* and *Down!*, always make sure that you are in control of a situation before you give a command to the dog. For example, do not tell a dog to *Sit!* when he is across the room. If he does not do as he's told, which is very likely if he doesn't completely understand the command, then you'll have to get up and place him in a sit. After this happens once or twice, your dog learns a lesson detrimental to your training program—that *he* is in control, not you, when he is out of arm's reach.

Obeying commands at a distance is something that you will teach the dog only when he understands the commands very well while he is at your side and only after he is accustomed to immediately obeying your commands.

Hide & Seek: A Game for in the House

Hide & Seek is a game that is fun for one dog and absolutely outrageous for a pack of dogs. The rules are pretty simple. Leave your dogs in a stay or have someone hold them. Then, run and hide somewhere in the house! When you're well hidden, call your dogs!

This is a great game for problem solving. Teach it to your dog while he's young and have fun with it forever.

Obstacles for Backyard Training: Jump and Dogwalk

Backyard Jump

For beginning canine jumpers, your jump should only be about 6" for little dogs or 12" for big dogs. Use a 5' piece of 1" i.d. PVC sitting on top of two cinder blocks.

Say *Jump!* and lead your dog over the jump. Immediately give a food treat.

If your dog refuses to jump, he does not get the food treat. Do not chastise the dog or otherwise make an emotional correction. That will not motivate the dog to come out and play agility. Simply withhold the treat and the praise. The dog will ultimately figure out what behavior earns the treat and praise, and what behavior earns him nothing. You must be very patient.

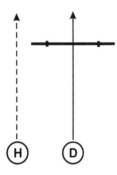

Work the dog on your right—the off-side position—until you are both comfortable. Give immediate praise and reward as the dog clears the jump.

During the initial stages of agility training, most handlers want to perform all obstacles with their dog in **heel position** (dog on your left). Here's an exercise you can start practicing at home that will hold you out from the crowd at class. This is an **off-side** jump, which means you start with your dog on your right side (opposite the traditional obedience or heel-side position) as shown in the illustration on the left. If you're accustomed to training and competing in obedience you may be reluctant to do this in competition. The solution is to do it in practice until both *you* and your dog are comfortable.

Backyard Dogwalk

Go to your local lumber yard and buy yourself a 2" x 12" board that is 12' long (or if you don't have a lot of room at your house get an 8' long plank). Get a pressure-treated board if you don't want it to warp. A treated board is a bit more expensive, but worthwhile in the long run.

Prop the board up on two cinder blocks. Make sure it's nice and sturdy with little or no wobble. Now you're ready to begin an "at home" dogwalk training program that will put you a step ahead of the competition.

For now you should use a lead in your training. At one end of the board give your dog a *Walk!* command and help him up on the board. Walk briskly with the dog to the other end of the board and give him a favorite food treat. Release the dog off the board with a quiet *Okay*.

NOTE: Do not give your dog a treat after he leaves the board. The treat should always be given while he's actually on the board! Also, do not use a ball or toy motivator when doing dogwalk training. The dog may perceive toys as a reward for getting off the board before you release him. That's not what you want to do in the early stages of training.

Week 2: Instructor Notes

It is always the instructor who adds the balance to a training plan to make it work. If you have extra time to fill, you give your students more repetitions. If you're running out of time, you cut down on the number of repetitions.

If your students, both human and canine, master the exercise too quickly, you might increase the difficulty and complexity of the exercise so they won't get bored. If your students are failing at the exercise, you will want to simplify it to give them more success and limit their frustration.

A good instructor is always ready to improvise depending on how an exercise is *or isn't* working.

All the while you address your students with a smile and an energetic persona. You motivate them to have fun with agility and encourage them to use the same attitude with their dogs.

Artist: Valerie Pietraszewska

	Jumps	Contacts	Poles/Table	Tunnels
Week 2	Review bar jump. Wing on one side and non-winged standard on the other. Little dogs 6"; big dogs 12". Introduce tire jump with tire resting on ground.	Review ladder. Review dogwalk at 3'.	Review weave poles with poles leaning so that tips are 12" off ground; gradually raise poles until they lean 45° off center. Introduce table at 6".	Review pipe tunnel. Start at 3' and work to full length. Begin bending one end into a curve. Introduce collapsed tunnel. Use only the barrel.

Organizational Notes

Review your Progress Worksheets from Week 1 to make note of the dogs that had control problems or obstacle problems. You should *not* let dogs with control problems off-lead in this class without very close supervision.

Remind your students that homework is important. If they can't build safe obstacles for their backyards, they should *at least* work on obedience exercises. Point out games and exercises in the Student Notes that don't require obstacles. Give each student a copy of a "A Philosophy for Training to Win" on pages 127–128.

Start the training session by doing the control exercise on page 29 with the entire group. Then break into groups for the training sets, if you're going to work multiple sets simultaneously. The training sets for this week include:

1. Review weave poles and introduce table

2. Review bar jump and introduce tire jump

3. Review dogwalk and ladder

4. Review pipe tunnel and introduce collapsed tunnel

Required Reading

The instructors should read:

- "A Philosophy for Training to Win" on pages 127–128.

- Exercises for Week 2 on pages 29–34.

Week 2: Progress Worksheet

Instructors: **Date:**

Handler and Dog	Attendance	Dogwalk	A-Frame	See-Saw	Weave Poles	Pipe Tunnel	Collapsed Tunnel	Bar Jump	Long Jump	Tire Jump	Table

GENERAL NOTES:

Week 2: Facility Layout

One square = 10'

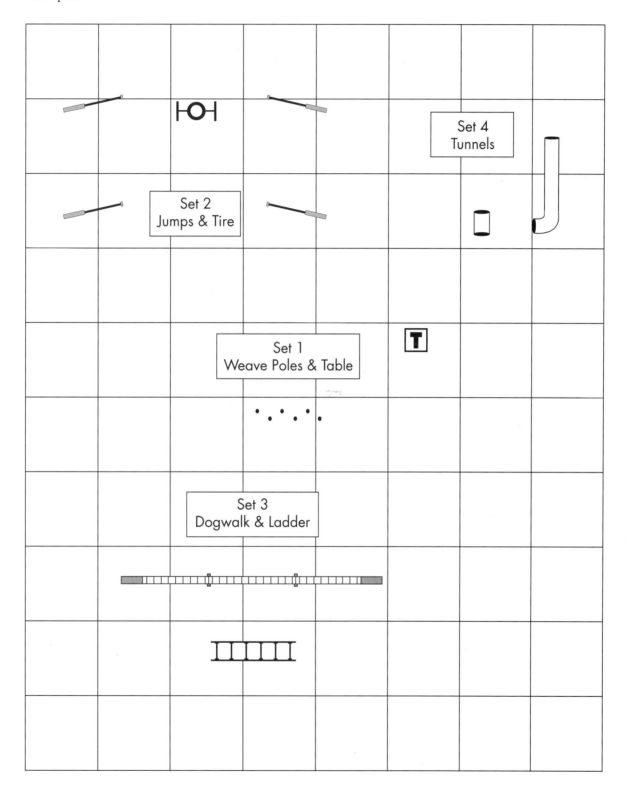

Set 4
Tunnels

Set 2
Jumps & Tire

Set 1
Weave Poles & Table

Set 3
Dogwalk & Ladder

Week 2: Facility Layout Worksheet

Design your Facility Layout using a 1" = 10' scale (standard agility template)

Introductory Agility Workbook

Week 2: Exercises

Start the class by doing the control exercise with everyone. Then break into smaller groups if you're going to work the training sets simultaneously.

Control Exercise

- Free heel the dogs into the field of equipment. (Dogs that demonstrated a control problem in Week 1 should be on-lead.) Allow them to sniff and to look at the equipment.

- Heel the dogs at attention into a long line. You need 8' to 10' between the dogs.

- *Down!* the dogs. Instruct handlers to leave their dogs and walk about 15', forming a line facing the dogs.

- Wait about 30 seconds (the instructor should keep time). If any dog breaks its stay during this time, the handler will collect the dog and hold on to it for the remainder of the exercise.

- Recall the dogs *one* at a time. Each handler commands his dog to *Come!* With any luck, the right dog will get up and come directly to the handler. If the dog does not, the handler will go and collect his dog. If the wrong dog comes, that dog's handler will collect his dog and put him back with the other dogs waiting to be recalled.

End of exercise. If any dogs are *not* coming to the handler, the instructor should demonstrate how to teach *Come!* using a long line, food, and praise. Make a note on your Progress Worksheet for dogs having difficulty.

Set 1: Review Weave Poles and Introduce Table

Your set consists of a set of weave poles and the table (a new obstacle). Plan on spending about half of your time with each group of students on each obstacle.

Review Weave Poles

Use a chute of six poles set up in a leaning poles configuration—first pole leans left, second pole leans right, and so forth, down the line. The poles are leaned away from center so the tips are no more than 12" above the ground. You are going to use a **bait plate** for this exercise. A bait plate can be a paper plate, a plastic bucket or coffee can turned upside down, or any other obvious target that won't get lost in the grass at an outdoor training facility. The instructor should be the baitmaster. Your job will be to place a treat on the plate for each dog and to be ready to snatch it away if the dog does the exercise incorrectly.

NOTE: Optionally, you can allow the handler to use a toy motivator or a food tube as a reward for the poles. Give the toy or food tube a short toss as the dog's nose emerges from the poles. Tossing the toy too early can entice the dog to cut out of the poles early.

Set 1
Weave Poles & Table

This exercise is performed on-lead.

1. With the dog on his left, each handler trots his dog down the chute of poles. Allow the dog to trot down the middle of the base. For dogs that are afraid of the base use a food or toy to help focus the dog as the handler leads him through.

2. Repeat step 1 but have handlers work the dog on their right.

3. When all dogs are comfortable, raise the poles slightly, and repeat steps 1 and 2.

4. Continue raising the poles, a few degrees at a time, and working the dogs on both sides until your time with the group is done. At no time in this class should the poles be raised higher than 45° off center.

End of exercise. Mark your worksheet for dogs having trouble.

Introduce Table

The table should be only slightly elevated, ideally to about 6". This exercise is performed on-lead.

This is an illustration of a pause table set at 30". The pause table you start training with should be much shorter. Computer Artist: Pascal Peng.

1. Trot the dog to the table and encourage him to hop up on it. Do *not* require the dog to sit or down on the table during his introduction to the obstacle.

2. Have each handler and dog team demonstrate a *Down!* on the ground *before* asking for a down on the table. Students that do not have a solid *Down!* away from the table should skip step 3. Homework for the "down-challenged" dog and handler team should include working on an obedience down as described in the Student Notes for Week 1.

3. Put each dog up on the table and immediately *Down!* the dog. Praise and treat the dog.

4. Release the dog off the table with an *Okay!* command.

ON A REFUSAL: If a dog is refusing the table, hold the dog on one side of the table and have the handler stand on the opposite side and call the dog up onto the table. If the dog is still having difficulty, the handler should sit on the table and call the dog to him. Praise and treat the dog.

End of exercise. Mark your worksheet for dogs having trouble.

Set 2: Review Bar Jump and Introduce Tire Jump

Your set is divided into two exercises: a review of the bar jump and an introduction to the tire jump. Plan on spending about half your time with each group of students on each exercise.

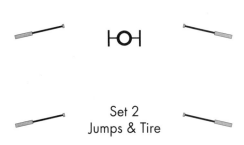

Set 2
Jumps & Tire

For a training jump, use a wing on the side away from the dog and handler so the wing isn't in the handler's way. Computer Artist: Pascal Peng.

Review Bar Jump

This exercise uses four bar jumps. Two are fixed with a wing on the left side and a narrow, non-winged standard on the other; the other two jumps are set up with a wing on the right side and a narrow standard on the other. Set the bars at 6" for little dogs and 12" for big dogs.

Elements of this exercise are performed off-lead.

We continue our goal from Week 1 to teach the dog to go between the jump standards on the handler's signal. Remind your students to square their bodies up for the obstacle, give a clear hand signal, and to have a food treat ready. Remember to use the treat *immediately* as the dog clears the bars of the hurdle and give the dog immediate and enthusiastic praise.

1. With the dog on his left, the handler trots the dog (on-lead) over the jumps with the wing on the left. Praise and reward.

2. With the dog on his right, the handler trots the dog (on lead) over the jumps with the wing on the right. Praise and reward.

3. Using either pair of jumps: The handler leaves the dog (*off-lead*), positions himself between the two jumps, calls the dog to him over the first jump, and then turns and trots with the dog over the second jump. If the dog will not stay while the handler moves away, have someone hold the dog.

4. Using either pair of jumps: The handler leaves the dog (*off-lead*), positions himself behind *both* jumps, and then calls the dog to him over the jumps. If the dog will not stay while the handler moves away, have someone hold the dog.

5. Repeat steps 1–4 two or three times each.

ON A REFUSAL: If a dog refuses a jump in step 1 or 2, this handler and dog team should not go on to step 3. Instead, the handler should take a remedial step. He should leave the dog on one side of the jump and take position on the opposite side of the jump, with the dog's lead passed over the bars, and encourage the dog over. Remember that praise and a food treat should be immediate and enthusiastic.

Introduce Tire Jump
Set the tire so that the bottom is resting on the ground. The goal is to teach the dog to jump through the tire.

• Demonstrate for your students how to square your body up for performance of the tire. Don't turn sideways to the dog. Face the tire and move directly toward it. Demonstrate a clear hand signal, using the hand closest to the dog, and pushing towards the tire.

• Remind your students to have a food treat ready in hand. Coach them to use the treat *immediately* as the dog goes through the tire. Give the dog immediate and enthusiastic praise.

This is an illustration of a regulation tire jump. Computer Artist: Pascal Peng.

Some elements of this exercise are performed off-lead.

1. If an extra body is available, assign a spotter to hold the dog on-lead at the entrance of the tire; otherwise the job is yours. Pass the dog's lead through the tire. The handler goes to the opposite side and entices the dog through with a food treat or toy motivator. Make sure each handler gets down and frames himself in the opening of the tire so he's visible to the dog. The handler should also stand back slightly from the tire so the dog has room to come through.

2. Repeat step 1 until the dog is happily diving through the tire.

3. With the dog on his left, the handler trots the dog (on-lead) towards the tire, releasing the lead as the dog enters the tire. Give praise and reward on the other side.

4. With the dog on his right, the handler trots the dog (on-lead) towards the tire, releasing the lead as the dog enters. Give immediate praise and reward.

5. The handler leaves the dog (*off-lead*), positions himself on the opposite side of the tire, and calls the dog to him through the tire. Again, make sure each handler positions himself so that he's visible to the dog. If the dog will not stay while the handler moves away, have someone hold the dog.

6. Repeat steps 1–5 until your time with this group is done.

End of exercise. Mark your worksheet for dogs having trouble with the tire jump.

ON A REFUSAL: The dog does not get the food treat. The handler should not chastise the dog or otherwise make an emotional correction. Simply withhold the treat and the praise. The dog will ultimately figure out what behavior earns a reward, and what behavior earns him nothing. Often a dog will refuse the tire because he is frightened or unsure. It is better with these dogs to be soothing and encouraging rather than forceful and demanding. Take the extra time to encourage the dog through.

Set 3: Review Dogwalk and Ladder

Your set consists of a ladder, laid flat on the ground, and the dogwalk elevated to 2' or 3'.

Review Ladder

The purpose of the ladder is to make the dog thoughtful of where he places his feet. Large dogs and younger dogs, especially, tend to be unaware of what their back feet are doing. Each handler walks his dog through the ladder (on-lead) two or three times. Make sure your students are leading their dogs through this exercise completely under control. No running!

Review Dogwalk

These instructions are based on the twelve-phase training program, "Walking the Plank: The Dogwalk", which is included in its entirety on pages 108–112. The instructions below are a summary of Phase 3 and Phase 4 of the program. The dog should be wearing a buckle collar and a tab for this exercise.

Set 3
Dogwalk & Ladder

1. Place a food treat at the bottom of the down plank and then lift the dog onto the *top of the down plank*.

2. Command the dog to *Walk!* and then guide him forward. The handler should signal to the waiting food. The handler should not use a verbal command like *Wait!*—the dog is expected to stop at the end of the plank of his own volition. If the dog does so, he gets food. If he doesn't stop, pick up the dog and put him back on the plank.

3. The dog is not permitted to leave the plank until the handler releases him with a quiet *Okay*.

4. Repeat steps 1–3 until the dogs are focusing on the end of the plank, anticipating the food reward, and waiting for release before leaving the plank. Do not continue to step 5 until you have achieved this! Dogs should advance as quickly as practical through the twelve phases of this program. However, they should advance only if they are being successful as described.

5. Place a food treat at the bottom of the down plank and then lift the dog onto the *middle of the center plank*.

6. Command the dog to *Walk!* and then guide him forward. If the dog stops at the end of the plank, he gets food. If he doesn't stop, pick up the dog and put him back on the plank.

7. As before, the dog is not permitted to leave the plank until released with a quiet *Okay*.

End of exercise. Mark your worksheet for dogs having trouble with the dogwalk.

ON A REFUSAL: If a dog is having trouble keeping all four feet on the dogwalk, the dog and handler should do some remedial work with the ladder. It would also be useful to set up a plank on some cement blocks so that they can work on their own while you continue working with the rest of the group. Suggest doing some motivational homework in the time before the next class. The handler needs to build a backyard dogwalk as described in the Student Notes for Week 1. During the week, the dog's meals should be quartered and each portion used to encourage the dog to walk the plank.

Set 4: Introduce Collapsed Tunnel and Review Pipe Tunnel

Your set will consist of the two types of tunnels used in agility: the collapsed tunnel and the pipe tunnel. Plan on spending about half of your time with each group of students on each obstacle.

To introduce dogs to the collapsed tunnel, you will use only the rigid portion of your collapsed tunnel. The chute should *not* be attached for this introduction.

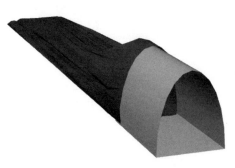

This is an illustration of a regulation collapsed tunnel with the full 12' chute that's used in competition. Computer Artist: Pascal Peng.

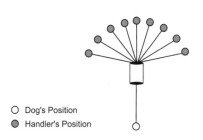

○ Dog's Position
● Handler's Position

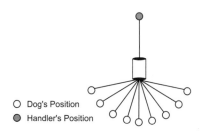

○ Dog's Position
● Handler's Position

Introduce Collapsed Tunnel

The emphasis in the following exercise is to make the dog understand what *the job* is. The job in performing any tunnel is for the dog to "find the hole", get in the tunnel, and pass through. The dog's angle of approach and the handler's position do not change the basic performance requirement—that is, the job.

Remind your students to have a food treat available. Coach them to use the treat and give enthusiastic praise immediately as the dog exits the tunnel.

This exercise is performed on-lead.

1. If an extra body is available, assign a spotter to hold the dog directly at the entrance of the tunnel; otherwise the job is yours. The handler goes to the opposite end of the tunnel, makes eye contact with the dog, and then calls the dog through. Give immediate praise and reward as the dog exits the tunnel.

2. In successive repetitions, the dog is left with the spotter at the six o' clock position (directly in front of the tunnel entrance). The handler, however, moves to different positions "around the clock" as shown in the illustration on the left. The handler should call the dog through using a voice command and a good hand signal. Give immediate praise and reward as the dog exits the tunnel.

3. If the dogs did well with step 2, try the exercise with the handler remaining stationary at the twelve o'clock position (directly in front of the tunnel exit). The spotter holds the dog at different positions around the clock and the handler calls the dog through the tunnel.

End of exercise. Mark your worksheet for dogs having trouble with the collapsed tunnel.

ON A REFUSAL: The dog does not get the food treat. The handler should not chastise the dog or otherwise make an emotional correction. That will not motivate the dog to come out and play agility. Simply withhold the treat and the praise. The dog will ultimately figure out what behavior earns the treat and praise, and what behavior earns him nothing.

If the dog is really adamant in his desire not to enter the tunnel he should not be forced. The handler of this dog needs to do some motivational homework in the time before the next class. The handler should take home a barrel for this homework. During the week, the dog's meals should be quartered and used to lure the dog through the barrel or short tunnel. This is an extremely effective method of curing a dog of tunnel shyness.

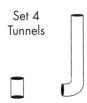

Set 4
Tunnels

Review Pipe Tunnel

Last week the dogs were introduced to the pipe tunnel compressed to no more than 3' in length. This week, begin with the compressed tunnel, but don't secure it because you will quickly expand the tunnel to increase its length (ideally you are using a 15' tunnel).

Remind your students to use a good hand signal to point to the tunnel's entrance and to have a treat ready for the dog so that they can give an immediate reward as the dog exits.

This exercise is performed on-lead.

1. Line up your students and then put the dogs through the tunnel on heel-side. Immediately treat and praise each dog as it goes through.

2. Increase the length of the tunnel by about 2' and repeat step 1. Continue gradually increasing the length of the tunnel for each successive repetition until the tunnel is stretched to its full length. For today, allow your students to work their dogs only on heel-side to increase the likelihood of success.

3. Once dogs are happily performing the tunnel at full length, gradually start bending the tunnel exit to the right (bending it this direction makes heel-side performance easier) until the dog is unable to see the exit end.

If a dog refuses the tunnel at any length, do the following:

• Have a spotter hold the dog at the entrance of the tunnel. The handler will get down at the exit end of the tunnel to establish eye contact and call the dog through.

• If the dog still refuses, have the dog and handler work with just the rigid portion of the collapsed tunnel instead of the pipe tunnel. Have a spotter hold the dog at the entrance and have the handler go to the other side of the barrel with bait or a toy. The handler should sit on the ground in a position where he's visible to the dog but not completely obstructing the opening (about 2' away). The spotter should pass the end of the dog's lead through to the handler and then move away. No pressure is ever exerted on the lead to force the dog through. The lead is simply a means of keeping the dog from backing away or running around the side of the tunnel. The dog now has two options: to stay right where he is or to go to the handler.

The handler shows his dog the lure but doesn't make a big fuss about convincing the dog to come through—he should just be patient and wait. Most dogs stop trying to get away when they realize they can't. They then start to get interested in the fact that the handler is sitting quietly on the other side of the tunnel with something they might want.

End of exercise. Mark your worksheet for dogs having trouble with the pipe tunnel.

Week 2: Student Notes

When teaching a dog to jump, you should raise his jump height only incrementally; say, an inch a week or an inch a month. The dog must learn to jump the higher bar not only with his muscles but with his brain. Don't be in a big hurry.

The worst case is the dog who has been routinely jumping 6" below his regulation height. Then, on the day the dog turns eighteen months of age, the handler raises the jump height the full remaining 6" and takes the dog to a show.

The handler *might* get away with this. It's more likely, on the other hand, that the dog and handler will have a long weekend, full of refusals.

Artist: Jo Ann Mather

Homework: *Go Around!*

This exercise is ideally performed using barrels. However, it could be done with trees, traffic cones, or stakes pounded in the ground. The objective of the exercise is to teach your dog to send away and go around the barrels.

Set the barrels about 20' apart. You stand in the middle. Send your dog out to go around one of the barrels, call the dog to come back to you, and then send the dog out to go around the other barrel. Piece of cake, right? Actually, you'll be amazed at how simple this is to teach your dog.

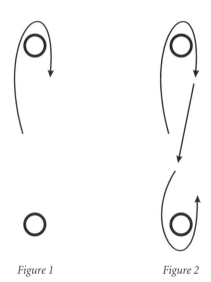

Figure 1   *Figure 2*

Follow these steps:

1. Initially, you will go out with your dog to each of the barrels. Use your dog's favorite treat to coax him around the barrel as shown in Figure 1. As soon as he goes around, you give enthusiastic praise and promptly give the treat. It's important that you don't go around the barrel. You have to remain on the inside, while the dog goes around the outside. (Who's training whom, after all!)

2. When your dog is happily going out around one barrel from 10' away, you will add the second barrel to the exercise. When the dog returns to you from the first barrel, pivot around, and send him to the second barrel as shown in Figure 2. As with the first barrel, you may initially have to go out with your dog to coax him around the second barrel.

3. Gradually put more distance between you and the barrel.

4. Start associating a command with the exercise—command your dog to *Go Around!*

Backyard Jumping

If you made yourself a backyard jump as described in the Student Notes for Week 1 and you worked on the jumping exercise from Week 1, then it's time to do something more advanced. For these new exercises, a Flexi-Leash™ may be helpful to direct the dog over the jump.

NOTE: When using any kind of lead with the dog, *always* give the dog enough slack to be able to perform the jump without being jerked away while committed in the air.

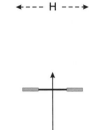

Figure 1

Call Over: Dog in Short Position

The exercise shown in Figure 1 positions the handler on the side of the jump opposite the dog.

You begin in a straight line and close to the jump. The dog should be positioned no more than 10' from the jump. Work in this fashion (every day, five or six minutes maximum) until the dog is performing without hesitating or refusing the jump.

Then, *gradually* move farther away from the jump and to one side or the other. The dog's starting position remains constant.

Figure 2

Call Over: Dog in Long Position

Begin the exercise illustrated in Figure 2 *only* after the dog has mastered the call over from the short position. Give a crisp hand signal and add a bit of body movement towards the jump. Start the dog near to the jump, but gradually move the dog farther back and position him at different approach angles to the jump.

Once the dog is adapting his approach path to the jump, regardless of the angle at which he is set up to approach the obstacle, then you can experiment with your own position, sliding to the left or right. Use your hand (in this case, the hand closest to the jump) to give the dog a signal to the jump. The hand acts like a flag, directing the dog towards the jump.

Call Over: Dog's Choice

Add a second jump to the call over exercise only after the dog has mastered the long position exercise. The exercise illustrated in Figures 3 and 4 will begin to tune your dog to your signals: your hand signal and use of body movement.

Position your dog as shown in Figure 3 and go to the other side of the jumps. You are going to alternately perform each jump, starting the dog from the same position each time. Give the dog a clear hand signal to the jump you want him to perform (use the hand on the same side as the appropriate jump) and slide laterally towards that jump. Once the dog is happily performing each jump, try the exercise in Figure 4.

Don't be distressed or impatient by early setbacks. If the dog attempts to come between the two jumps, stand closer to the jumps when you begin the exercise. Remember, you and your dog are learning to communicate: You are learning to use a clear and unambiguous signal; your dog is learning to interpret and act on that signal.

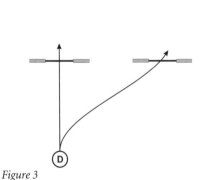

Figure 3

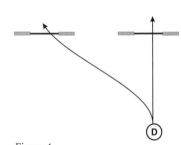

Figure 4

Introductory Agility Workbook

Week 3: Instructor Notes

The safety of all the dogs in class is your responsibility. This is the philosophy by which we engage in this sport. Here are some important tips for you:

Artist: Bud Houston

- Always inspect the equipment you will be using before class starts. Do not assume that someone has done it for you. You should be familiar with the safe operation of the equipment. Inspect used/worn equipment for dangerous developments.

- Watch the dogs for signs of heat, overwork, and dehydration. Do not assume that handlers are aware of their dogs' limits. You are an instructor. So instruct.

- Aggressive dogs should *not* be allowed in mixed training. Be very keen to spot trouble before it turns into injury. Be firm. Send the aggressive dog *home*.

	Jumps	Contacts	Poles/Table	Tunnels
Week 3	Review bar jump. Non-winged jumps. Little dogs 6"; big dogs 12". Review tire. Little dogs tire on ground; big dogs 12".	Review ladder. Review dogwalk at 3'. Introduce A-frame elevated to 3' at apex.	Review weave poles with poles leaning 45° off center. Review table at 6".	Review curved pipe tunnel, graduating to "U" shape. Review collapsed tunnel. Add 3' chute and gradually lengthen.

Organizational Notes

Review the Progress Worksheets from Week 2. Identify for your instructors those dogs that are most likely to have trouble, especially with the tire and the tunnels. It might be a good idea to group together dogs having problems with these obstacles.

Start the training session by doing the control exercise on page 41 with everyone. Then break into groups for the training sets, if you're going to work multiple sets simultaneously. Your working sets for this week are:

1. Review weave poles and table

2. Review bar jump and tire jump

3. Review dogwalk and ladder and introduce A-frame

4. Review tunnels

Required Reading

The instructors should read:

- "Training the A-Frame" on pages 113–115.

- Exercises for Week 3 on pages 41–47.

Week 3: Progress Worksheet

Instructors: **Date:**

Handler and Dog	✓ Attendance	Dogwalk	A-Frame	See-Saw	Weave Poles	Pipe Tunnel	Collapsed Tunnel	Bar Jump	Long Jump	Tire Jump	Table

GENERAL NOTES:

Week 3: Facility Layout

One square = 10'

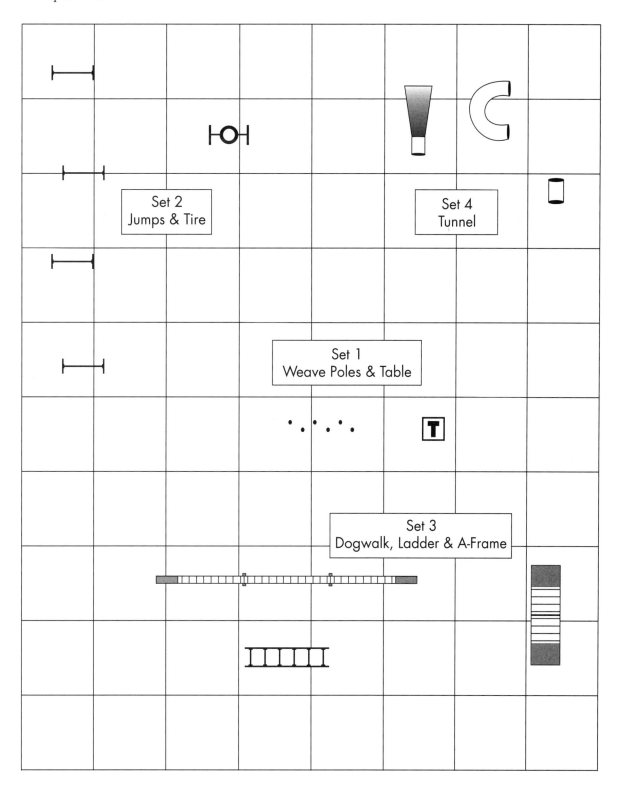

Set 2
Jumps & Tire

Set 4
Tunnel

Set 1
Weave Poles & Table

Set 3
Dogwalk, Ladder & A-Frame

Week 3: Facility Layout Worksheet

Design your Facility Layout using a 1" = 10' scale (standard agility template)

Week 3: Exercises

Start the class by doing the control exercise with everyone. Then break into smaller groups if you're going to work the training sets simultaneously.

Control Exercise

- Free heel the dogs into the field of equipment. (Dogs that demonstrated a control problem in Week 2 should be on-lead.) Allow them to sniff and to look at the equipment.

- Heel the dogs at attention into a long line. You need 8' to 10' between the dogs.

- *Down!* the dogs. Instruct handlers to leave their dogs and walk about 15', forming a line facing the dogs.

- Wait about 30 seconds (the instructor should keep time). If any dog breaks its stay during this time, the handler will collect the dog and hold on to it for the remainder of the exercise.

- Recall the dogs *one* at a time. Each handler commands his dog to *Come!* With any luck, the right dog will get up and come directly to the handler. If the dog does not, the handler will go and collect his dog. If the wrong dog comes, that dog's handler will collect his dog and put him back with the other dogs waiting to be recalled.

End of exercise. If any dogs are *not* coming to the handler, remind those handlers to continue working on their *Come!* command at home using a long line, food, and praise. Make a note on your Progress Worksheet for dogs having difficulty with control.

Artist: Jaci Cotton

Set 1: Review Weave Poles and Table

Your set consists of a set of weave poles and the table. Plan on spending about half of your time with each group of students reviewing the obstacles and the other half with working on the weave poles-to-table sequence.

Set 1
Weave Poles & Table

Review Weave Poles

Uses a chute of six poles set up in a leaning poles configuration—first pole leans left, second pole leans right, and so forth, down the line. The poles are leaned away from center so the tips are about 45° off center (this is exactly halfway between a straight upright position and lying flat on the ground). Continue to use a bait plate at the end of the weave poles as you did in Week 2. The instructor should be the baitmaster.

This exercise is performed on-lead.

1. Trot each dog down the length of poles with the dog on the handler's left. Allow the dog to get the treat from the bait plate and give him praise.

2. Repeat step 1 with the dog working on the handler's right.

Table Instructions

Set the table at 6". This exercise is performed on-lead.

1. Put each dog up on the table and give him praise and a treat while still on the table. Do *not* ask the dog to lie down.

2. Linger only a moment and then release the dog off the table with an *Okay!* command.

Weave Poles to Table Sequence

Put the table about 12' from the end of the weave poles and put the bait plate on the table. The last step of this exercise is performed off-lead; all other steps are performed on-lead.

1. With the dog on his left, have each handler trot his dog through the poles and then put the dog up on the table to get the treat. Do *not* ask the dog to lie down.

2. With the dog on his right, have each handler trot his dog through the poles and then put the dog up on the table to get the treat. Do *not* ask the dog to lie down.

3. Repeat steps 1 and 2 until all dogs are comfortable.

4. Place the bait plate on the table. Allow the dog to go *off-lead* through the chute of poles and put the dog up on the table.

   NOTE: If the dog cuts out of the poles, the baitmaster should immediately remove the bait so the dog isn't rewarded. The dog should be put back on-lead for the remainder of the set.

5. If you have time, do the weave poles *off-lead*, put the dog up on the table and let him get the food reward, and then quickly *Down!* the dog. Have the dog stay down two or three seconds before praising and releasing.

End of exercise. Mark your worksheet for dogs having trouble with the poles or the table.

Set 2: Review Tire and Bar Jump

Your set consists of the tire jump and a series of four non-winged bar jumps. Review the tire first, allowing each handler to put his dog through twice, and then move on to the sequence of jumps for the balance of your time with the group.

At this time in your training, there will be dogs that are having difficulty with the tire. Allow the handlers of these dogs to do the jump sequence once or twice; then instruct them to spend the rest of their time with the tire. Use treats and a lot of happy voice motivation with these dogs. The work *must* be on-lead until the dog is happily performing the tire.

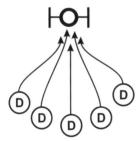

Review Tire Jump

Raise the tire 12" for big dogs; keep it resting on the ground for little dogs. Remind your students to have a food treat available. The first steps of this exercise are performed on-lead and then the dog is allowed off-lead.

1. With the dog on his left, the handler trots the dog toward the tire, releasing the lead as the dog enters. Give immediate praise and reward.

2. Repeat step 1 working with the dog on the handler's right.

3. The handler leaves the dog (*off-lead*), positions himself on the other side of the tire, and calls the dog through the tire. Make sure each handler positions himself so that the dog can see him through the opening of the tire. If the dog will not stay while the handler moves away, have someone hold the dog.

4. Working *off-lead*, begin directing the dog to the tire in an "around the clock" fashion as you did with the collapsed tunnel in Week 2. The dog's job is to find the hoop. The dog is left with a spotter at the six o' clock position (directly in front of the tire). The handler, however, moves to different positions "around the clock". The handler should call the dog through using a voice command and a good hand signal. Give immediate praise and reward as the dog comes through the tire.

5. If the dogs did well in step 4, try the exercise with the handler remaining stationary at the twelve o'clock position (directly in front of the tire exit). The spotter holds the dog at different positions around the clock and the handler calls the dog through the tire.

End of exercise. Mark your worksheet for dogs having trouble with the tire.

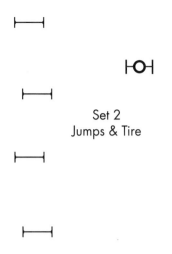

Set 2
Jumps & Tire

Review Bar Jump

Sequencing is basic to agility. Work this line of jumps in sequence. Keep the jumps *very* low (6" for little dogs; 12" for big dogs) so that you don't stress the dogs. Encourage your students to use lots of praise and treats. Place a bait plate at the end of the line of jumps. The baitmaster should snatch the treat away if a dog runs *around* any of the jumps. Try the exercise both on-lead and off-lead.

1. Experiment with the handler running the sequence with the dog on his left as well as with the dog on his right.

2. Experiment with the handler calling the dog over two jumps and then pushing the dog ahead to the remaining jumps.

End of exercise. Mark your worksheet for dogs having trouble.

Set 3: Review Dogwalk and Ladder and Introduce A-Frame

Your set consists of a ladder, laid flat on the ground, and the dogwalk elevated to 2' or 3'. You also have a new obstacle to introduce—the A-frame.

Review Ladder

The purpose of the ladder is to make the dog thoughtful of where he places his feet. Large dogs and younger dogs, especially, tend to be unaware of what their back feet are doing.Each handler walks his dog through the ladder (on-lead) two or three times. Make sure your students are leading their dogs through this exercise completely under control. No running!

Unless you have dogs that are still having trouble keeping their rear end on the dogwalk plank, this will be the last time you use the ladder in conjunction with the dogwalk.

Set 3
Dogwalk
A-Frame & Ladder

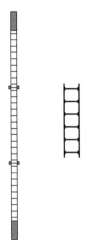

Review Dogwalk

These instructions are based on the twelve-phase training program, "Walking the Plank: The Dogwalk", which is included in its entirety on pages 108–112. The instructions below are a summary of Phase 5 and Phase 6 of the program. At first, the dog should be wearing a 6' lead so you can easily control the dog if he fails to stop for the food reward at the end of the plank.

1. Place a food treat at the bottom of the down plank and then start the dog *from the ground* at the beginning of the dogwalk.

2. Command the dog to *Walk!* and allow him to ascend the plank. The handler should signal to the waiting food at the end of the plank. The handler should not use a verbal command like *Wait!*—the dog is expected to stop at the end of the plank of his own volition. If the dog does so, he gets food. If he doesn't stop, pick up the dog and put him back on the end of the plank.

3. The dog is not permitted to leave the plank until the handler releases him with a quiet *Okay*.

4. Repeat steps 1–3 until the dogs are focusing on the end of the plank, anticipating the food reward, and waiting for release before leaving the plank. Do not continue to step 5 until you have achieved this!

5. Repeat the entire exercise (steps 1–4) with the dog *off-lead*.

End of exercise. Mark your worksheet for dogs having trouble.

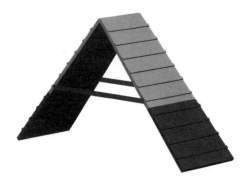

This is an illustration of a full-height A-frame. Your students will be introduced to this obstacle elevated to about 3', perhaps supported by a sawhorse. Computer Artist: Pascal Peng.

Introduce A-Frame

Introduce the A-frame elevated to 3'. Students will bait the down contact of the A-frame *each* time they put their dog over. This exercise should be performed with a buckle collar and tab.

1. Place a food treat on the lowest slat of the down ramp and then lift the dog onto the *center of the down ramp*. The handler should signal to the waiting food to encourage the dog to focus downward to the end of the ramp. The handler should *not* use a verbal command like *Wait*—the dog is expected to stop at the end of the ramp of his own volition. If the dog does so, he gets food. If he doesn't stop, pick up the dog and put him back on the ramp.

2. Place a food treat on the lowest slat of the down ramp and then start the dog on the ground at the *beginning of the A-frame*. Have the handler coax his dog up the ramp with a food motivator. A spotter on the opposite side should assist. The spotter should have a *loose* hold on the dog's buckle collar or tab. Encourage the dog to climb.

3. As the dog reaches the apex, give lots of praise. Allow the dog to continue forward to the downside contact zone to get the food reward. The dog is *not* required to stop at the apex.

   NOTE: A common problem is that as the dog nears the top of the A-frame, he will lean backward on the spotter's hand in the collar. Do not allow the dog to do this. The purpose of the hand in the collar is only to prevent the dog from turning around, not for support. Make the dog do the work. Do *not* allow the dog to turn and descend the ramp if he gets frustrated; merely lift him off if he seems truly unable to climb. If this is the case, the A-frame must be lowered further.

4. The dog is not allowed to leave the A-frame until the handler releases him with a quiet *Okay*. Handlers should not praise or feed the dog, or celebrate as the dog leaves the plank—*positive reinforcement should occur only in the contact zone.*

ON A REFUSAL: If the dog has difficulty climbing the ramp or tries to jump off, it may be necessary to demonstrate to the dog that he must reach forward with a paw to gain purchase on a slat. In this case, move each paw for the dog and use lot of treats to encourage the dog.

All dogs should be confident in climbing the A-frame slat-by-slat because there are many instances where the dog may not have momentum to assist him. In addition, dogs that don't understand how to scale the A-frame using the slats may start jumping too high onto the up ramp when they approach the obstacle. As the height of the A-frame is raised, many of these dogs start missing the up-side contact zone.

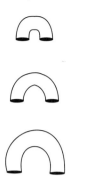

Start the pipe tunnel review by compressing the tunnel into a small "U" shape with the openings close together. Keep expanding the tunnel into a bigger "U" shape and moving the openings farther away from each other.

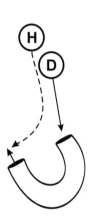

Set 4: Review Tunnels

In this set you will review both of the tunnels. The collapsed tunnel will have a chute attached for the first time. This tunnel requires a spotter whose job will be to gradually add length to the fabric chute with each successive repetition, and also to open the chute to allow reluctant dogs to see through.

Review Pipe Tunnel

Your objective with this exercise is simply to get the dogs moving to and through the tunnel happily and reliably. It is very important for the handler to have a treat in his hand ready for the dog.

Last week you left off with the tunnel by gradually introducing a bend in the end of it. This week begin with a slightly curved tunnel and quickly graduate the curve until the tunnel is shaped in a small "U". Then work on making the "U" bigger as shown on on the left. Using the "U" shape allows the handler to send the dog into the tunnel and to be right there at the exit to give the dog an immediate reward. This exercise is performed *off-lead*.

1. Put the dogs through the slightly curved tunnel on heel-side. Immediately treat and praise each dog as it goes through.

2. Repeat step 1 working the dogs on the right.

3. Continue working this way, graduating the curve on each repetition until the tunnel forms a small "U". On each repetition, alternate the side on which the dog is working.

4. When dogs are happily performing the tunnel as a small "U", start expanding the tunnel so that the "U" gets bigger.

5. Do this exercise until everybody has had enough.

End of exercise. Mark your worksheet for dogs having trouble.

Review Collapsed Tunnel

In this exercise a spotter should be used to gradually add length to the fabric chute of the tunnel with each successive repetition. Begin with about a 3' chute. This exercise is performed on-lead.

1. Put the dogs through the tunnel on heel-side. Immediately treat and praise each dog as it comes through the chute.

2. Repeat step 1 working the dogs on the right.

3. Continue working this way, increasing the length of the chute about 1' with each repetition. On each repetition, alternate the side on which the dog is working.

End of exercise. Mark your worksheet for dogs having trouble.

ON A REFUSAL:

- Have a spotter hold the dog at the entrance of the tunnel. The handler should get down on the ground at the exit end, lift the fabric chute open to establish eye contact, and call the dog through. If the spotter makes the dog nervous, pass the lead through to the handler.

- Shorten the fabric.

Introductory Agility Workbook

Week 3: Student Notes

It is far better to train smart than it is to train long. A dog that's forced to work an hour or two a day is likely to learn to dislike this sport. If you can work with your dog twice a day (or even twice every other day) for only ten minutes at a time, you will make the most of his capacity to learn.

Use the dog's regular meal as incentive to play agility with you. Divide his dinner into six portions. Now, send him out over a jump to get each portion! This works best if you have someone in position to take away the food if he fails to go over the jump.

Over time, you can modify this approach to get a few extra repetitions out of the dog. Give him the food treat at irregular intervals. In other words, he might get the food twice in a row and not get it the third time; or, get the food once and not get it the next two times. This motivates the dog to do the exercise even when he doesn't find any food. In his mind, he knows that it's worth doing simply because he *might* get some food.

Artist: Karen Gaydos

Obstacles for Backyard Training: Weave Poles

The easiest kind of poles to make are ones that you stick in the ground. Cut steel rebar into 2' long pieces and drive them into the ground at regular intervals (between 18" to 24"). Now, slide a 3' long piece of 3/4" i.d. PVC pipe over each section of rebar. Remember how you do weave poles in class? You should do the same at home: When you stick the poles in the ground, the first pole leans left, the second pole leans right, and so on down to the end of the line.

If you don't have enough yard space to do weave pole training, you could do it in the house. For example, you could purchase six bathroom plungers and make a weave pole chute down the hallway. Instead of leaning the poles, you just stagger them left and right. Over time you would slowly bring the poles together to form a straight line. Just don't be in a big hurry!

Two Poles

This exercise is performed with two free-standing weave poles. The poles should be spaced 22" apart.

The objective of the exercise is to teach your dog to send away and to go between the two poles, passing from the right side of the poles, past the first pole, to the left side of the poles. The dog should then curl around the second pole (left to right) and return to you.

1. Initially, you will go out with your dog to coax him between the two poles with a treat. As soon as he goes through, back up quickly, give enthusiastic praise, and give the treat.

2. Gradually put more distance between you and the poles, until you can send your dog between the poles from about 6' away.

3. Start commanding your dog to *Go Weave!* when you send him to the poles.

4. When your dog is happily going out between the two poles and returning to you, begin changing the angle from which you send your dog to the poles.

Do this exercise for a week or two. Remember to *constantly* and *consistently* make the exercise very fun. You want the dog to relish the performance and to look forward to the easily earned treats.

Bowling for Goodies: A Game for in the House

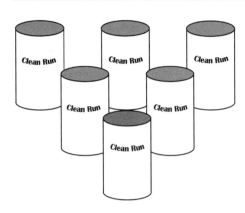

Here is a fun game for the house—especially in a long hallway—that will: a) provide hours of amusement for you and your house guests; b) give you and your dog something to do when it's snowing outside; c) work on your repertoire for *That's My Dog*; and d) teach your dog something useful that is related to agility.

Start with a simple cardboard canister, ideally a 1 lb. oatmeal container or a Stovetop Stuffing™ container. Place a piece of your dog's favorite food treat or his favorite stuffed toy underneath the canister. Allow him to see you doing this, but hold him by the collar because he's going to want to investigate. Then, when you're ready, say *Go!*, and release him to knock down the canister and retrieve the treat or toy.

Now, increase the complexity of the exercise. Arrange a group of similar canisters into a bowling pin configuration. Hide the motivator under *one* of the canisters, but don't let the dog see which one. It's the same exercise as when there was only one canister. Hold your dog at a distance. Release with a *Go!* command and a good hand signal (pantomime releasing a bowling ball). Keep score if you like.

Safety Tip: Don't use aluminum cans or tin cans for this game—they're not safe because they have sharp edges.

A Very Special Treat: Liver Muffins

If your dog is having trouble with a particular exercise or obstacle, it frequently helps to "up the ante". You need to convince the dog that the potential payoff is going to be worth tackling the job. This may require a *really* special food treat.

The following recipe has been passed among dog trainers for a number of years, although no one seems to know where it originated. In any event, liver muffins make an excellent treat. They break apart easily, they don't make a mess in your pocket, you can freeze them and just thaw one or two as needed, and the dogs love them!

Puree in blender:

- 1 lb. raw liver (any kind—chicken is the least expensive)
- 3 eggs
- 3 tbsp. blackstrap molasses

Dry ingredients:

- 2 $^1/_2$ cups whole wheat flour
- 1 tsp. baking soda
- At least 1 tbsp. garlic powder
- At least 1 tbsp. onion powder

The following optional dry ingredients can be used to produce the muffin consistency you desire. You can add about a $^3/_4$ cup of one, or a combination of several, to the ingredients above:

- wheat germ
- bran
- bulgar wheat
- brewer's yeast
- parsley

Add the blended mixture to the dry ingredients and stir until just mixed. Place in greased muffin tins (do not use muffin cups as they will not peel off the muffins). Bake at 350° for about 20 minutes. Makes 18 muffins.

Making a Food Tube

There are many training situations where it's desirable to be able to throw an object for your dog to get as a reward for doing an exercise correctly—for example, to speed up a dog in the weave poles you can throw a ball as the dog weaves the last two poles; or, to get your dog to go away from you over a jump, you can throw a frisbee for the dog to chase over the jump. People who have dogs that aren't toy-motivated feel they can't take advantage of these training methods—but this is not the case at all. One option for a dog that isn't toy-motivated is to make a holder for your treats that you can throw. This holder allows the dog to see and smell the treats, but he can't actually get a treat without your help. One such popular holder is an object commonly referred to as a **food tube**. A food tube is easy and cheap to make!

Shopping List
- A length of Clear Vinyl Tubing. Even small hardware stores sell this type of tubing by the foot (cost is around $1.00 to $1.25 per foot). You can usually find it in the aisle where they have copper tubing and other sorts of plumbing pipe. Buy the size marked 7/8" o.d., 5/8" i.d. , and 1/8" wall thickness. If you buy several feet, you can make a few food tubes at a time.

- Two 7/8" rubber furniture tips (sometimes called chair, cane, or crutch tips) for each food tube you plan on making (cost is around .25 to .45 each).

Making the Tube
1. Use an X-acto knife or a cardboard cutter to cut the tubing into pieces. The length of the pieces depends on your personal preference—a 6" or 8" long piece works well for medium and large dogs; a 4-1/2" piece works best for small dogs, but can also be used with a larger dog and offers the convenience of fitting in your pocket.

2. Cut a 3" *diagonal* slit across the center of the tube. Your cut should go through only one layer of the tubing.

3. Place a furniture tip on each end of the tube.

Using the Tube
To open the tube, hold the tube with one hand on each end. The slit should be facing upwards. Now twist the ends of the tube in opposite directions. The slit opens up so you can remove a treat when the tube is filled.

To "load" the tube with treats, just take off one of the end caps and fill it up. Make sure that you break up the treats into small enough pieces that they fit in easily (this means they'll be easy to get out as well!).

Introducing the Tube to the Dog
It's a good idea to put your dog on-lead to introduce him to the food tube since the first instinct of many chow-hounds is to grab the tube and run for a comfortable spot where they can shred it and get the food out! Wave the tube around to get him interested in it and then toss it about a foot or two from the dog. If the dog makes any attempt to pick up the tube, or even if he just noses or paws at it, make a big fuss and give him a treat from the tube. Do this a few times. If the dog isn't picking up the tube, delay giving him a reward from the tube—allow him a little more time to explore and experiment to see if he'll pick the tube up on his own. If your dog does pick up the tube, give the dog a *Give!*, *Out!*, or *Drop It!* command and gently remove the tube from the dog's mouth. Immediately remove a reward from the tube for the dog. As the dog gets the idea, start asking him to bring the tube towards you—use the lead to gently encourage him to come to you. Again, with a dog that doesn't have strong retrieving instincts, you should initially reward the dog just for taking a few steps towards you. While having the dog actually retrieve the tube isn't a requirement of using the food tube, it is useful and saves a lot of wear and tear on you! Some dogs will gleefully chase the food tube but will wait where you've thrown it, wagging their tails and waiting for you to come to their aid. In these cases, you'll have to go out to where the tube lands to reward the dog.

NOTE: Food tubes are for training sessions only! Never leave your dog unattended with access to the food tube and never allow the dog to play by himself with the food tube.

Homework: *Lie Down!*

For this exercise, get out that special food treat that your dog would die for. Do *not* use a toy. You are going to teach your dog to *Lie Down!* on command. This exercise is in four parts and is typically not something that you are going to accomplish in a day. Give yourself and your dog several days—or weeks if necessary—to master each part before moving on to the next. These exercises will pay great dividends later in your agility training.

Part 1

1. Put your dog on-lead and take him on a short walk.

2. Standing in front of your dog with the treat ready in hand, say *Lie Down!* Immediately reach down to the ground, under the dog's chin, with the treat. This forces the dog to get on his belly to get the treat. You might have to give him an assist with your left hand as you offer the treat with your right hand.

3. Release your dog. Praise your dog. End of exercise.

4. Walk awhile with your dog at your side and then repeat the exercise. Do this over and over again until your dog anticipates the down. Then proceed to Part 2.

Part 2

1. Give your dog the *Lie Down!* command. As he anticipates the reward, he will drop to his belly. Wait a second or two, then reach down to the ground, under the dog's chin, and give the treat.

2. Release your dog. Praise your dog. End of exercise.

3. Walk awhile with your dog at your side and then repeat the exercise. Do this over and over again until your dog is holding the down consistently as you wait. Then proceed to Part 3.

Part 3

1. Give your dog the *Lie Down!* command. As he anticipates the reward, he will drop to his belly. Wait five seconds, then reach down to the ground, under the dog's chin, and give the treat.

2. Gradually increase the amount of time you wait before giving the treat. You want your dog to reliably maintain the down position for 15 or 20 seconds.

3. Release your dog. Praise your dog. End of exercise.

4. Walk awhile with your dog at your side. Then do the exercise again. Do this over and over again until your dog is holding the down consistently as you wait. Then proceed to Part 4.

Part 4

1. Give your dog the *Lie Down!* command. As he anticipates the reward, he will drop to his belly.

2. Walk a step or two away from your dog. Wait five seconds. Then return to your dog, reach down to the ground under the dog's chin, and give the treat.

3. Gradually increase the distance that you put between you and your dog before returning with the treat. You would like to walk as many as ten paces away while your dog holds the down position.

4. Release your dog. Praise your dog. End of exercise.

5. Walk awhile with your dog at your side and then repeat the exercise. Do this over and over again until your dog is holding the down consistently no matter where you walk and how long you wait.

Week 4: Instructor Notes

Here are some more safety tips for you:

- Leads are used for controlling the dog. Choke collars or pinch collars should *not* be allowed at the training site. Do *not* allow handlers to haul their dogs over the equipment using the lead in a forceful manner.

- When introducing dogs to contact equipment, or their first time at full height, use spotters. A spotter's job is to catch the dog when it steps off the board and plummets towards the ground. So, the spotter should be physically capable of catching the dog. The spotter must also be *prepared* to catch the dog. More than one dog has been injured because the spotter was taken by surprise. Don't be surprised.

Artist: Jo Ann Mather

TIP FOR SPOTTERS: Watch the dog's *feet* on the contact obstacle rather than the handler or the dog's upper body. Watching the feet allows you to anticipate a misstep before the dog actually falls off the obstacle. Very often you can keep the dog from falling and correct his path simply by putting your hands on his hips to keep his legs moving within the confines of the width of the plank.

	Jumps	Contacts	Poles/Table	Tunnels
Week 4	Review bar jump. Non-winged jumps. Little dogs 6"; big dogs 12". Review tire. Little dogs tire on ground; big dogs 12". Introduce long jump. Two planks, bar jump between.	Review dogwalk at 3'. Review A-frame at 3' and then raise to 4'.	Review weave poles with poles leaning 45° off center. Review table at 6".	Review pipe tunnel in "U" shape. Review collapsed tunnel with 4' chute.

Organizational Notes

Review the Progress Worksheets from Week 3. You should discuss problem dogs with your instructors prior to class so that they are mentally prepared to help these animals. It is important that the training experience be a positive experience. Remind your instructors that you do *not* use force to make a dog commit to an obstacle.

Start the training session by doing the control exercise on page 55 with everyone. Then break into groups for the training sets, if you're going to work multiple sets simultaneously. Your working sets for this week are:

1. Forked sequence

2. Speed circle and introduce long jump

3. Review dogwalk and pipe tunnel

4. *Come!* and *Go!* sequence

Week 4: Progress Worksheet

Instructors: **Date:**

Handler and Dog	✓ Attendance	Dogwalk	A-Frame	See-Saw	Weave Poles	Pipe Tunnel	Collapsed Tunnel	Bar Jump	Long Jump	Tire Jump	Table

GENERAL NOTES:

Introductory Agility Workbook

WEEK 4

Week 4: Facility Layout

One square = 10'

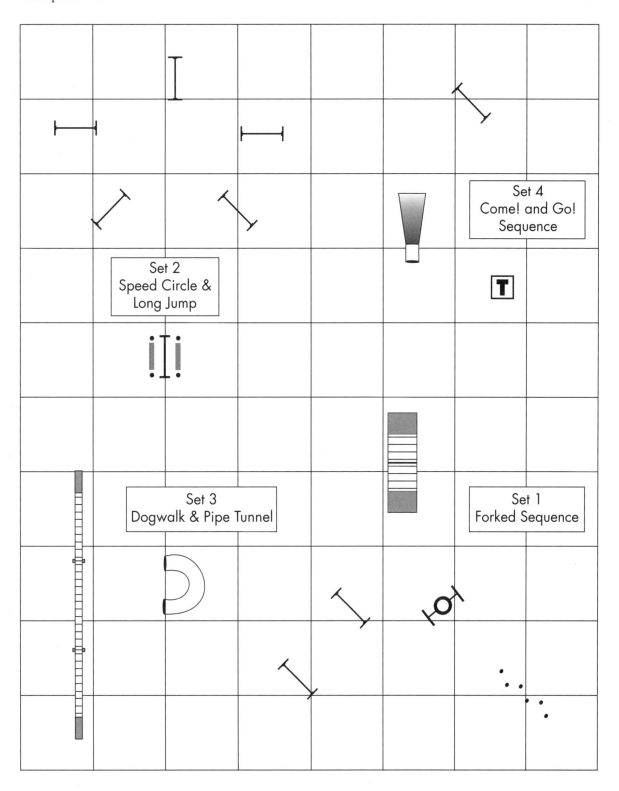

Set 4
Come! and Go!
Sequence

Set 2
Speed Circle &
Long Jump

Set 3
Dogwalk & Pipe Tunnel

Set 1
Forked Sequence

Week 4: Facility Layout Worksheet

Design your Facility Layout using a 1" = 10' scale (standard agility template)

Introductory Agility Workbook

Week 4: Exercises

Start the class by doing the control exercise with everyone. Then break into smaller groups if you're going to work the training sets simultaneously.

Control Exercise

- Free heel the dogs into the field of equipment. (Dogs that demonstrated a control problem in Week 3 should be on-lead.) Allow them to sniff and to look at the equipment.

- Heel the dogs at attention into a long line. You need 8' to 10' between the dogs.

- *Down!* the dogs. Instruct handlers to leave their dogs and walk about 15', forming a line facing the dogs.

- Have the handlers turn and, in line, march around to one end of the line of dogs. The line of handlers should then weave in and out between the dogs.

- Instruct your students to return to their dogs. Praise and release.

Set 1: Forked Sequence

In this set, you will review the tire, weave poles, and A-frame individually. You will then run a sequence using all of these obstacles and some jumps.

Review Tire Jump
Raise the tire to 12" for big dogs; keep it resting on the ground for little dogs. Remind your students to have a food treat ready. This exercise is performed *off-lead*.

1. With the dog on his left, the handler briskly heels the dog to the tire. Coach your students to give a clear *Tire!* command and use the arm closest to the tire to point into the tire aperture.

2. Repeat step 1 with the dog working on the handler's right.

3. The handler leaves the dog, positions himself on the opposite side of the tire, and calls the dog to him through the tire. Make sure each handler positions himself so that the dog can see him through the opening of the tire. If the dog will not stay while the handler moves away, have someone hold the dog.

Review A-Frame
The A-frame should be elevated to 3'. This exercise is performed with a buckle collar and tab.

1. Have the handler place a food treat on the lowest slat of the down-side contact zone. If possible, let the dog see the handler placing the treat.

2. With the dog on the handler's left, trot the dog up and over.

3. The handler should allow the dog to get the food and then release the dog off the A-frame with a quiet *Okay*. Remember, if the dog doesn't stop for the treat or if he leaves the obstacle before the handler releases him, pick up the dog and put him back on the ramp.

4. Repeat steps 1–3 working the dog on the handler's right.

5. Raise the A-frame to 4' and repeat the entire exercise (steps 1–4).

ON A REFUSAL: If any dog has difficulty with the A-frame, lower the height of the obstacle.

Review Weave Poles

Uses a chute of six poles set up in a leaning poles configuration—first pole leans left, second pole leans right, and so forth, down the line. The poles are leaned away from center so the tips are at about a 45° angle (this is exactly halfway between a straight upright position and lying flat on the ground). Continue to use a bait plate at the end of the weave poles as you did in Week 3. The instructor should be the baitmaster.

The last step of this exercise is performed off-lead. All other steps are performed on-lead.

1. Trot each dog down the length of poles with the dog on the handler's left. Allow the dog to get the treat from the bait plate and give him praise.

2. Repeat step 1 with the dog working on the handler's right.

3. Repeat steps 1 and 2 one more time.

4. Allow the dog to go *off-lead* through the chute of poles.

    NOTE: If the dog cuts out of the poles, the baitmaster should immediately remove the bait so that the dog isn't rewarded. Put the dog back on-lead for one repetition.

5. If you have time, add a new exercise: Leave the dog on a stay (off-lead) at the entrance to the poles. Have the handler trot down to the end of the poles and call the dog through.

Set 1
Forked Sequence

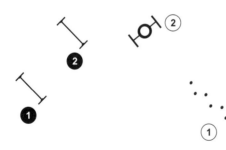

Forked Sequence

After reviewing the individual obstacles, alternately perform the following sequences until your time with the group is done:

* Weave poles, tire, and then A-frame

* Jump, jump, and then A-frame

The jumps should be set at 6" for little dogs and 12" for big dogs. For each repetition, make sure that you bait the last slat in the down-side contact zone of the A-frame.

NOTE: Do *not* reverse the direction of these sequences and start on the A-frame. At this point in their training, your students should not be pushing their dogs off the A-frame to another obstacle—you do not want the dog to perceive going to another obstacle as a reward for leaving the contact zone.

These sequences provide a great opportunity to work on basic handling skills. Each handler should:

* Square up his body with the direction of the flow.

* Use a good hand signal.

* Give a clear and early voice command.

Mark your worksheet for dogs having trouble with the tire, the A-frame, or the weave poles.

Set 2: Speed Circle and Introduce Long Jump

Your set consists of a sequence of jumps arranged in what is referred to as a speed circle and the long jump—a new obstacle for this week.

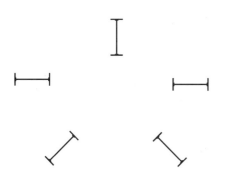

Speed Circle

The jumps should be set at 6" for little dogs and 12" for big dogs. This exercise is performed *off-lead*.

- This is a speed and enthusiasm drill. The handler should be very upbeat with a slow dog and make liberal use of praise and treats to encourage the dog to move quickly around the circle.

- This set offers the opportunity to work with the dog on both sides with the handler in the middle of the jumps.

- A circle is a constant change of direction. Suggest that handlers use *Come!* to turn the dog's path into the circle.

Run the speed circle until your students have had enough. Be sure to alternate directions with each repetition.

Mark your worksheet for dogs having trouble with the jumps.

Introduce Long Jump

The practice long jump should be quite short—use only two 6" or 8" panels. To make the dogs appreciate that they have to jump the entire span, put a bar jump between the two panels. The bar jump should be set at 6" for little dogs and 12" for big dogs.

Remind your students to have a food treat readily available. The first steps of this exercise are performed on-lead and then the dogs are allowed off-lead.

NOTE: The instructions are the same even if you are using a broad jump rather than a long jump.

This is an illustration of a regulation long jump set in an ascending fashion. In competition, the long jump is adjusted for the jump height of the dog. The length of the long jump is usually double the dog's jump height. Computer Artist: Pascal Peng.

1. With the dog on his left, have each handler trot his dog up to and over the obstacle. Give immediate praise and reward.

2. Repeat step 1 with the dog working on the handler's right.

3. The handler leaves the dog in a sit (*off-lead*) in front of the long jump, positions himself on the opposite side of the jump, and calls the dog to him over the jump. If the dog will not stay while the handler moves away, have someone hold the dog. Remind the handler that he should still be working on stays with the dog at home.

End of exercise. Mark your worksheet for dogs having trouble with the long jump.

Set 3: Review Dogwalk and Pipe Tunnel

Your set uses the dogwalk (elevated to 2' or 3') and the pipe tunnel (in a "U" shape) in separate exercises. Divide your time evenly between each of these obstacles.

Review Dogwalk

These instructions are based on the twelve-phase training program, "Walking the Plank: The Dogwalk", which is included in its entirety on pages 108–112. The instructions below are a summary of Phase 7 and Phase 8 of the program. Handlers should have a food reward ready in hand rather than leaving it at the end of the down plank. This exercise is done *off-lead*.

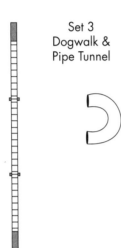

Set 3
Dogwalk &
Pipe Tunnel

1. Start the dog *from the ground* at the beginning of the dogwalk.

2. Command the dog to *Walk!* and allow him to ascend the plank. The handler should signal to the end of the plank with his inside hand (the hand closest to the dog), actually touching the end of the down plank. As the dog approaches the zone, *wait for the dog to pause,* and then *immediately* place the food on the end of the plank.

   The handler should carry the food in his outside hand; that is, the hand farthest away from the dog and the dogwalk. The handler should not use a verbal command like *Wait!*—the dog is expected to stop at the end of the plank of his own volition. If the dog does so, he gets food. If he doesn't stop, pick up the dog and put him back on the plank.

   NOTE: If the dog leaves the dogwalk before reaching the contact zone, you can put the dog back on the plank at the point where he left it. The handler should put his hand in the dog's collar and lead the dog to the end of the plank. Then reward the dog for being in the zone.

3. The dog is not permitted to leave the plank until the handler releases him with a quiet *Okay*. Do not ask the dog to do additional obstacles yet.

4. Repeat steps 1–3 until the dogs are focusing on the end of the plank, anticipating the food reward, and waiting for release before leaving the plank. Do not continue to step 5 until you have achieved this!

5. Repeat the entire exercise (steps 1–4), *gradually* increasing the interval of time that elapses before the handler places the food reward on the end of the plank. Also, encourage the handler to begin increasing the distance he works from the dog. Your students should always follow a parallel path to the dogwalk until they reach the end of the plank and they should always place the food on the plank.

WEEK 4

Review Pipe Tunnel

As in Week 3, the emphasis in this exercise *remains* on making the dog understand what the job is: to "find the hole", get in, and pass through. We add to the challenge the *possibility* that the handler may ask the dog to perform another obstacle in sequence after the tunnel. This exercise will also teach the dog to be aware of the handler's signal when performing a sequence. Dogs should be *off-lead* for this exercise.

In the illustration below, the numbers outside the tunnel indicate the handler's starting position and approach path to the tunnel. From each of these positions (beginning with 1 and working to 7), the handler will send the dog to the tunnel and then alternately A) send the dog over the jump; and B) call the dog back. So, for example, beginning at position 1, each handler will send his dog through the tunnel, over the jump, and then reward. In the next repetition, each handler will send his dog through the tunnel from position 1, call the dog to him as it exits the tunnel, and then reward. The exercise is then repeated from position 2 and so on.

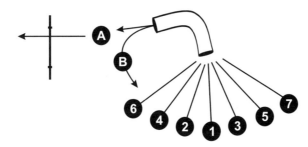

The handler does not have to stay at the numbered approach path after committing the dog to the tunnel. In fact, the handler should meet the dog as he exits the tunnel to give the dog the next command—either to proceed over the jump or to come to the handler.

End of exercise. Mark your worksheet for dogs having trouble with the pipe tunnel.

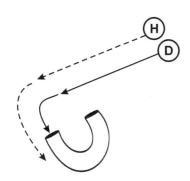

Alternate Tunnel Exercise

Try this alternate exercise with your group if there is enough time. The objective of the exercise is to introduce dogs to the idea that the tunnel is to be performed only when the handler asks (commands) that it be performed. It's a good idea to break up routine tunnel work with this exercise.

This exercise is performed on-lead.

With the tunnel in a "U" shape, each handler heels his dog past the first opening to the tunnel as shown in the illustration on the left. Then, the handler abruptly turns and signals the dog to perform the tunnel. Praise and reward as the dog exits.

Set 4: *Come!* and *Go!* Sequence

Your set uses the collapsed tunnel with the chute extended to 4', a jump set at 6" for little dogs and at 12" for big dogs, and the pause table set at 6" for all dogs.

This exercise gives your students an opportunity to work on *Come!* versus *Go!* and helps teach their dogs to listen. Your students will alternate performing the following two sequences:

•   Table, tunnel, jump, table

•   Table, tunnel, table

This exercise is performed *off-lead*.

1. Start the dog on the table.

2. Working with the dog at his side, the handler should use a *Come!* command after the tunnel when performing the table-tunnel-table sequence; and he should use a *Go Jump!* command after the tunnel when performing the table-tunnel-jump-table sequence.

3. Finish each repetition by putting the dog back on the table.

NOTE: The handler should use treats and reward the dog only when the dog does what the handler asks.

Initially, have your students reward any thoughtful performance of the obstacles. Before too long, however, you should have them withhold treats for any refusal (the dog stops prior to either the collapsed tunnel or the jump) since you don't want to reinforce refusals. The dog will figure out why the treat is being withheld only so long as handlers are consistent with the reward.

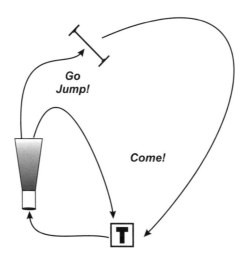

Set 4
Come! and Go!
Sequence

Week 4: Student Notes

By now, you have probably observed that dogs progress at different speeds. There are some dogs in class who work as though they've been doing this sport forever. Other dogs are slower and don't seem to be enjoying themselves. Often these dogs need to be shown something several times before they understand the task.

Even if your dog is doing well right now, you need to prepared for the ups and downs of learning. One week your dog may do great on the A-frame; then the next week, he's fearful of the obstacle and acts like he's never seen it before.

The key is to be patient with your dog. If you are in a big hurry, you might push your dog along faster than he is ready to go and *possibly* turn him off of this sport.

- Use praise, food treats, toys, and a lot of patience.

- Progress only as fast as your dog is willing.

- Never make an emotional correction.

- Don't fret over how slowly your dog learns. The important thing is that he *does* learn and he enjoys coming out with you to play.

Artist: Nancy Krouse-Culley

More Backyard Jumping

Hopefully, you have been practicing the jumping exercises from the previous weeks' Student Notes! If so, here's another one to add to your repertoire. For this exercise, you are going to need a food tube or some other "dog-safe" container that you can put treats in. The reason for the container is that you need a way of preventing the dog from getting a treat if he does the exercise incorrectly.

Set up two jumps about 15' apart. Keep the jumps low; at this point in your training, you shouldn't be worried about seeing how high your dog can jump. The goal of this exercise is to teach your dog that, when commanded, he can leave your side and go perform an obstacle on his own. This skill is often referred to as a **send-away**.

1. Let the dog sniff the food tube or whatever treat holder you've decided to use so that he knows you have something good for him. Then, place your food target as shown in the illustration below (about 10' away from the jump). Hold your dog by the collar or on leash and let him go with you to place the target.

2. Standing next to your dog behind the first jump (initially, start very close to the jump), command your dog to *Go Jump!* Let your dog go over the jump without you running next to him—you stay behind the jump.

3. When your dog gets to the target you placed, go out and give him a reward from the container and praise.

4. Repeat steps 1–3 a few times.

5. During the week, repeat the exercise for five or ten minutes at a time. On subsequent repetitions, start the dog from farther behind the first jump (only move back a foot or so at a time). If at any point, your dog expresses hesitation about jumping, stop moving back and work on send-aways from the same starting position until the dog is performing enthusiastically. Don't be in a hurry! Gradually keep moving back until you can send your dog to the food target from behind the second jump.

NOTE: If the dog runs around a jump, he doesn't get the reward. Don't chastise him or make a correction. Walk him up to the target, let him see it, and tell him that he missed out on a really great treat! Then try the exercise again.

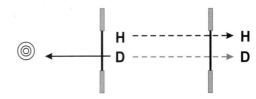

Teaching an Instant Down

If your dog is slow to lie down when commanded, try this technique for teaching the dog an "instant" down. In an instant down, the dog "collapses" his body into the down position rather than taking his time and gradually lowering his body to the ground. This technique is also useful for re-adjusting your dog's attitude if he is reluctant to lie down when commanded. The idea is to make this a fun game rather than a battle of wills.

The following can be done outside on dry grass or inside during a t.v. commercial break if you prefer!

WEEK 4

1. Kneel down on the ground. Keeping your right knee on the ground, make a "tunnel" with your left leg by bending it and putting your foot on the ground (swap legs if you're more comfortable working in the other direction).

2. Use a treat to get the dog's interest—entice him a bit but don't let him have the treat.

3. Hold the dog by the collar, if necessary, to keep the dog on one side of your raised leg. With your other hand, hold the treat under your raised leg on the side opposite the dog—make sure the dog can see it. Encourage the dog to get the treat but do not give him any verbal commands.

   NOTE: It might take awhile to get your dog to play this game. Make it clear that the only way he's going to get the cookie is to go underneath your leg. Don't make any corrections or give the dog any commands. Just encourage him.

4. As the dog starts to go under your leg, pull the food away so the treat is always just at the end of the dog's nose. Keep moving the treat away until the dog comes all the way through the "tunnel" as shown in the picture on the left. Praise the dog and let him have the treat.

5. Repeat steps 1–4 until the dog is happily and quickly going under your leg for the treat.

6. Now we start working on getting the dog into a down. To do this, you need to figure out at the correct position for your leg—the key is for your leg to be at the height that forces the dog into an immediate down position when he dives through for the treat. For a small or medium dog, you may need to sit on the ground as shown in the picture on the left. For a large dog, the position you've been using may work fine.

7. Again, hold the dog on one side of your raised leg and hold the treat under your leg on the side opposite the dog—make sure the dog can see it. Encourage the dog to get the treat.

8. As the dog starts to go under your leg, pull the food away so the treat is always just at the end of the dog's nose. Keep moving the treat away until the dog comes all the way through the "tunnel". Praise the dog and let him have the treat.

Once your dog is *gleefully* playing the game, you can start reinforcing the down verbally. When the dog dives through into the down position and gets the treat, say "Good Down!" or whatever word you want to use. It's important to give the dog the treat as soon as he's down each time. You want him to figure out that the faster he gets down, the faster he can teach you to give him the treat!

Week 5: Instructor Notes

We hold great store in the application of reward, whether it be praise, a food treat, a "click", or a favorite toy. By application of this reward, the dog learns to distinguish between doing a task right and doing it wrong.

Your job will be to teach your students to *consistently* give a *well-timed* reward. Well-timed usually means giving the reward immediately so that you are reinforcing *correct* performance. Remind your students to have the reward ready and to give it immediately. If they have to dig through their pockets for the reward or fumble around opening a bait bag, the moment for teaching the dog that he has done the task right has past.

Conversely, give a gentle correction to your students for giving arbitrary and pointless reward, especially if a handler is feeding or praising a dog for being disobedient or for ignoring him.

Artist: Valerie Pietraszewska

The opposite of reward is correction. Again, consistency is key to a dog's learning. We do *not* support harsh physical or emotional corrections. An incorrect performance can be communicated to the dog by withholding the reward. That's all. Consistent application of reward creates a powerful communication link between handler and dog. The handler can clearly tell the dog "yes" or "no". The dog will understand and will learn more quickly.

	Jumps	Contacts	Poles/Table	Tunnels
Week 5	Review bar jump. Winged and non-winged jumps. Little dogs 6"; big dogs 12". Review tire. Little dogs tire on ground; big dogs 12". Review long jump. Little dogs: two planks, bar jump between, 20" spread; big dogs: three planks, two bar jumps between, 30" spread.	Review dogwalk at 3'. Review A-frame at 4'. Introduce see-saw with no plank motion.	Review weave poles with poles leaning 40° off center. Review table. Little dogs 6"; big dogs 12".	Review pipe tunnel in various configurations. Review collapsed tunnel with 8' chute.

Organizational Notes

Review the Progress Worksheets from Week 4. Identify for your instructors those dogs most likely to have trouble with individual obstacles. If necessary, group together dogs having problems with specific obstacles.

Start the training session by doing the control exercise on page 67 with everyone. Then break into groups for the training sets, if you're going to work multiple sets simultaneously. Your working sets for this week are:

1. First dogwalk sequence and weave pole review

2. Change of direction jumps

3. Attacking the A-frame

4. Introduce see-saw and review table, collapsed tunnel, and long jump

Required Reading

The instructors should read:

- "Training the See-Saw" on pages 116–123.

- Exercises for Week 5 on pages 67–72.

Week 5: Progress Worksheet

Instructors: Date:

Handler and Dog	Attendance	Dogwalk	A-Frame	See-Saw	Weave Poles	Pipe Tunnel	Collapsed Tunnel	Bar Jump	Long Jump	Tire Jump	Table

GENERAL NOTES:

Week 5: Facility Layout

One square = 10'

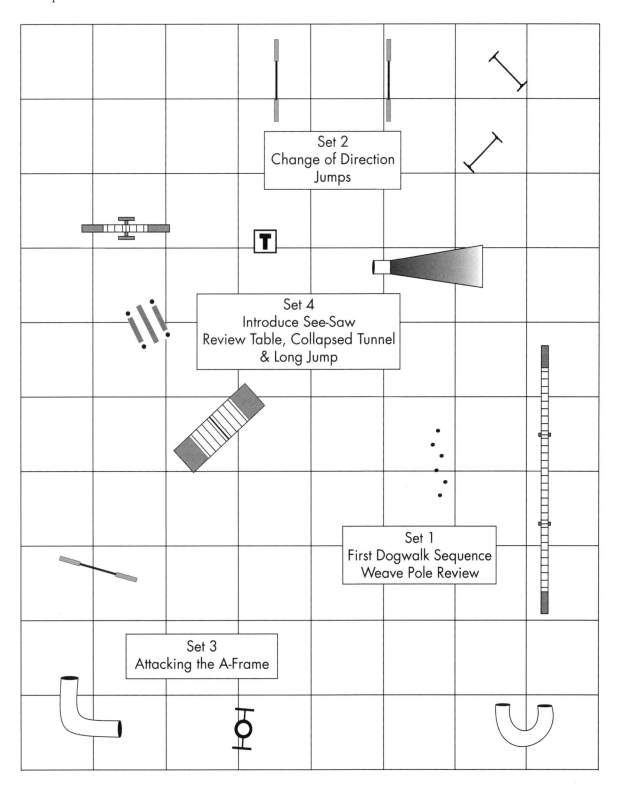

Set 2
Change of Direction
Jumps

Set 4
Introduce See-Saw
Review Table, Collapsed Tunnel
& Long Jump

Set 1
First Dogwalk Sequence
Weave Pole Review

Set 3
Attacking the A-Frame

Week 5: Facility Layout Worksheet

Design your Facility Layout using a 1" = 10' scale (standard agility template)

Introductory Agility Workbook

Week 5: Exercises

Start the class by doing the control exercise with everyone. Then break into smaller groups if you're going to work the training sets simultaneously.

Control Exercise

- Have your students free heel their dogs into the field of equipment. Don't work in a line—allow them to go where they will. Allow the dogs to sniff and to inspect the equipment, but keep the dogs off the equipment.

- Instruct the handlers to stop wherever they are, down their dogs, and to leave their dogs.

- Have handlers walk around the field, walking close to the other downed dogs. If any dog breaks its stay, that dog's handler should return to the dog and put it *back* in a down.

- Instruct the handlers to find a spot at least 30' away from their own dogs.

- One at a time, each handler calls his dog. Praise and hold on to the dog until everyone has done the exercise.

End of exercise.

Set 1: First Dogwalk Sequence and Weave Pole Review

Your set consists of the dogwalk (elevated to 2' or 3'), a pipe tunnel ("U" shape), and a set of leaning weave poles.

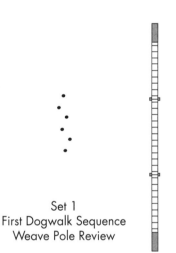

Set 1
First Dogwalk Sequence
Weave Pole Review

Review Dogwalk

These instructions are based on the twelve-phase training program, "Walking the Plank: The Dogwalk", which is included in its entirety on pages 108–112. The instructions below are a summary of Phase 9 and Phase 10 of the program. Handlers should have a food reward ready in hand. The dogs should be *off-lead* for this exercise.

1. Start the dog *from the ground* at the beginning of the dogwalk.

2. Command the dog to *Walk!* and allow him to ascend the plank. The handler should signal to the end of the plank. The handler should *not* use a verbal command like *Wait*—the dog is expected to stop at the end of the plank of his own volition. If the dog doesn't stop, pick him up and put him back on the plank at the point he left it.

3. Once the dog has paused, release him with a quiet *Okay, Walk!* command.

4. Give the food reward *two steps beyond* the end of the plank.

NOTE: This exercise teaches the dog that it's permissible to leave the plank without a food reward, if he is *commanded* to do so. Do not repeat this step multiple times as it contradicts the basic premise of this program, which is to reward the dog only for being in the contact zone.

First Dogwalk Sequence

Set up a pipe tunnel in a "U"-shaped configuration about 10' from the end of the down plank. Place a food reward on the down plank and also have food in hand. This exercise is performed *off-lead*.

1. Place a food reward at the end of the down plank and then start the dog *from the ground* at the beginning of the dogwalk.

2. Command the dog to *Walk!* and allow him to ascend the plank. The handler should signal to the waiting food. The handler should not use a verbal command like *Wait!*—the dog is expected to stop at the end of the plank of his own volition. If the dog does so, he gets food. If he doesn't stop, pick the dog up and put him back on the plank at the point he left it.

3. Once the dog has paused and been rewarded, release him with a quiet *Okay, Tunnel* command. Remember, the dog is not permitted to leave the plank until released.

4. Give the dog quiet praise and a food reward as the dog exits the pipe tunnel.

Review Weave Poles

Use a chute of six poles set up in a leaning poles configuration—first pole leans left, second pole leans right, and so forth, down the line. The poles are leaned away from center *beginning* at a 45° angle. You will work on raising the poles until they are 40° off center. Continue to use a bait plate at the end of the poles as you did in Week 4. The instructor should be the baitmaster.

Dogs will be *off-lead* for this exercise.

1. With the dog on the handler's left, trot each dog down the chute of poles. If the dog cuts out, he should be put *back* on-lead for one or two repetitions.

2. Repeat step 1 with the dog working on the handler's right. If the dog cuts out he should be put *back* on-lead for one or two repetitions.

3. Repeat steps 1 and 2 until all dogs are comfortable, but for each repetition raise the poles *incrementally* (only an inch or two at a time). If the dogs are cutting out, set the poles at the last angle you used where the dogs had the most success.

4. If you have time: Leave the dog on a stay at the entrance to the poles. Have the handler trot down to the end of the poles and call the dog through.

Set 2: Change of Direction Jumps

The jumps should be set at 6" for little dogs and 12" for big dogs. Dogs will be *off-lead* for this exercise.

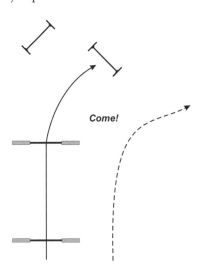

Come!

The jumps are set in a curve mainly because it allows the handler to take a short path while the dog takes the longer path. This means that the dog must hurry to keep up when the handler begins running. From the very beginning you want to encourage the dog to move briskly.

The illustration on the left shows both the path of the dog (solid line) and the path of the handler (dashed line). Notice that the handler's path turns sharply and early. The faster the dog, the more critical it will be for the handler to make an early turn. If the handler pushes too far into the pocket of jumps, the fast dog will push out over the dummy jump.

A slower dog that watches his handler's every movement will tend to stay at the handler's side, which will probably require the handler to turn much closer to the side of the final jump than is shown in the illustration.

Set 3: Attacking the A-Frame

Your set consists of the A-frame, the tire, a pipe tunnel, and a jump. You will review each obstacle with your students, as outlined below, before beginning the "Attacking the A-Frame" sequence. Don't get your students too carried away with the idea of *attacking*. Actually, you want a very controlled performance of the A-frame at all times. Make sure that there is always bait in the down-side contact and that dogs are not allowed to leave the obstacle until the handler has given a quiet release command.

Set 3
Attacking the A-Frame

Review A-Frame

For this exercise, the A-frame should be elevated to 4-1/2'. This exercise is performed off-lead.

1. Have the handler place a food treat on the lowest slat of the down-side contact zone. If possible, let the dog see the handler placing the treat.

2. With the dog on the handler's left, trot the dog up and over.

3. The handler should allow the dog to get the food and then release the dog off the A-frame with a quiet *Okay*. Remember, if the dog doesn't stop for the treat or if he leaves the obstacle before the handler releases him, pick up the dog and put him back on the ramp.

4. Repeat steps 1–3, working the dog on the handler's right.

Review Tire Jump

The tire should be set at ground level for little dogs and at 12" for big dogs. Remind your students to have a food treat available. This exercise is performed *off-lead.*

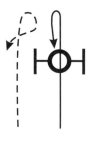

1. With the dog on his left, the handler briskly heels the dog to the tire. Coach your students to give a clear *Tire!* command and use the arm closest to the tire (and the dog) to point into the tire aperture.

2. Repeat step 1 with the dog working on the handler's right.

3. The handler leaves the dog, positions himself on the other side of the tire, and calls the dog through the tire. Make sure each handler positions himself so that the dog can see him through the opening of the tire. If the dog will not stay while the handler moves away, have someone hold the dog.

4. Next, the handler should approach the tire with the dog on his right. The handler should send the dog through the tire, immediately turn towards the dog (so that the dog is now on the handler's left), and put the dog back through the tire. Praise and treat the dog after the second time through.

Review Pipe Tunnel

Beginning with a "U"-shaped tunnel, do this exercise to emphasize the use of hand signals. Thie exercise is performed *off-lead.*

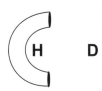

1. Position the handler in the curve of the tunnel between the two entrances. The dog is left on a stay, just a few feet away, in a straight line with the handler. The handler gives a strong hand signal to the left or right tunnel entrance (using the hand closest to the entrance he wants the dog to take) and commands *Tunnel!* This helps get the dog used to performing obstacles coming towards the handler and also works on the handler's hand signals.

2. Now, change the exercise so that the handler and dog start together in the middle of the tunnel, a few feet away from the obstacle, as shown in the illustration on the left. Again, the handler should give a strong hand signal to the left or right tunnel entrance and command *Tunnel!* Alternately have the handler start the dog from the heel-side position and from the off-side position.

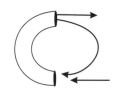

3. Once again have the handler and dog start together in the middle of the tunnel, a few feet away from the obstacle. First, the handler sends the dog into the left entrance. As the dog emerges from the tunnel, the handler should immediately wheel him back around to the *original* entrance, and then send him through the tunnel again as illustrated on the left. Give the dog a treat and praise only after the second trip through the tunnel.

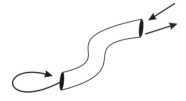

4. Set up the tunnel in an "S" configuration as shown in the illustration on the left. Put each dog through the tunnel. As the dog exits, turn the dog around and put it through the tunnel again. Give the dog a treat and praise only after the second trip through the tunnel.

WEEK 5

70   Introductory Agility Workbook

Attacking the A-Frame

This *off-lead* exercise presents the A-frame in a sequence that will build up speed in the dogs, if they are comfortable with the obstacles. The apex of the A-frame should be set at no more than 4'; the jump should be set at 6" for little dogs and 12" for big dogs; and the tire should be set at ground level for little dogs and at 12" for big dogs.

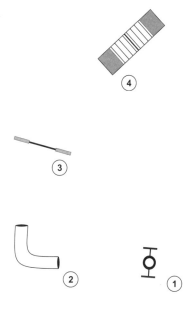

- Each handler should place a treat on the down-side contact of the A-frame before starting the sequence. Also remind everyone to give a release word before allowing the dog to leave the A-frame. The objective is *not* to go fast, but to perform the obstacle reliably.

- This sequence features an overall and gradual change of direction. This is a good opportunity to talk to your students about using *Come!*. Any time the direction changes for the dog, the handler should signal that change to the dog.

- As your students repeat this sequence, it should be possible for the handler to take a shorter path. For instance, it should not be necessary for the handler to run all the way to the pipe tunnel if the dog is running at the tunnel and happily committed to it.

- Do *not* reverse the direction of the flow in this set. These dogs are not ready to perform an obstacle after the A-frame.

Set 4: Introduce See-Saw and Review Long Jump, Tunnel, Table

Your set consists of the see-saw (a new obstacle); the long jump; a tunnel; and the table. You will *not* do any sequencing with these obstacles, but rather review them individually.

Introduce See-Saw

These instructions are based on the training program, "Walking the Plank: The Teeter", which is included in its entirety on pages 116–123 in the Appendix. The instructions below are a summary of Phase 1 and Phase 2 of the program. The dog should be wearing a buckle collar and a short tab for this exercise. A spotter on the side opposite the handler may be useful to steady the dog and increase its sense of security. The teeter does *not* move in this phase of training.

Side A

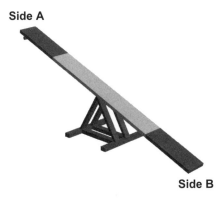

Side B

This is a regulation see-saw with no slats attached to it. Many agility organizations do not require the see-saw to have slats. Computer Artist: Pascal Peng.

1. Lift the dog onto *the Side B end* of the plank, facing downward off the teeter, and reward him with food and praise for remaining there. The dog can be in any position but standing is preferred. At first, give the food directly to the dog; then place it on the end of the plank. The handler should signal to the food by pointing to it with the hand closest to the dog, encouraging the dog to focus downward to the end of the plank.

2. The dog is not permitted to leave the plank until the handler releases him with a quiet *Okay*. Handlers should not praise or feed the dog, or celebrate as the dog leaves the plank. *Positive reinforcement should occur only in the contact zone.* The exercise ends when the dog leaves the see-saw plank. You may restart the exercise.

   ON A REFUSAL: If the dog attempts to leave the plank, say nothing. Pick up the dog and put him back on the end of the plank. Reward the dog again for being in the contact zone. With some dogs, you may need to do this a few times. Do not get angry at the dog; just keep replacing the dog on the plank until he is willing to wait for a release command.

3. Repeat this exercise until the dogs are focusing on the end of the plank, anticipating the food reward, and waiting for release before leaving the plank. Do not continue to step 4 until you have achieved this!

4. Place a food treat at the bottom of the down plank and then lift the dog onto *the center of the plank*, facing downward off the teeter, towards the Side B end of the plank.

5. Command the dog to *Walk!* and then guide him forward. The handler should signal to the waiting food. The handler should not use a verbal command like *Wait!*—the dog is expected to stop at the end of the plank of his own volition. If the dog does so, he gets food. If he doesn't stop, pick up the dog and put him back on the end of the plank.

   NOTE: If you prefer to have your students use different commands for the dogwalk and the see-saw, use a word other than *Walk!* in these steps.

6. As before, the dog is not permitted to leave the plank until released with a quiet *Okay*.

Review Table

Set the table at 6" for little dogs and 12" for big dogs. This exercise is performed *off-lead*.

1. The handler should place a food treat on the table.

2. The handler puts the dog up on the table and allows the dog to get the treat.

3. Immediately after the dog gets the treat, the handler should *Down!* the dog for a count of three seconds, then treat, release, and praise the dog.

4. Repeat steps 1–3. This time challenge your students to hang back as their dog goes on to the table. If the dog won't advance beyond the handler, then the handler should immediately move in towards the table and put the dog up on the obstacle.

Review Collapsed Tunnel

Use an 8' chute. This exercise is performed *off-lead*.

1. The handler should briskly approach the tunnel with the dog in heel position and give the *Tunnel!* command.

2. The handler should briskly approach the tunnel with the dog in the off-side position and give the *Tunnel!* command.

Remind your students to use a good hand signal, pointing down to the tunnel opening with the hand closest to the dog and tunnel. Also, your students should be talking to their dogs while the dog is in the fabric chute. The movement of the handler's voice will encourage the dog to move through the chute.

Review Long Jump

For little dogs, use a 6" jump between two long jump planks, with about a 20" spread. For big dogs, use two 12" bar jumps shuffled between three planks, with about a 30" spread. This exercise is performed off-lead.

1. Have the handler leave the dog in a sit-stay about 20' from the long jump. The handler takes up position about halfway to the long jump, to the right of the line the dog will take to the long jump. The handler should turn slightly and command his dog to *Come!* and then *Over!* Remind your students to get their hand (the one closest to the dog) out like a flag.

2. Have the handler leave the dog in a sit-stay about 20' from the long jump. Again the handler takes up position halfway to the long jump, but this time he stands to the left of the path that the dog will take to the jump. The handler again turns slightly and commands the dog to *Come!* and then *Over!*

3. Have the handler leave the dog in a sit-stay about 20' from the long jump. This time the handler moves to the far side of the long jump and commands the dog to *Come!* and then *Over!*

Week 5: Student Notes

If you really get bitten by the agility bug, it's almost certain that before too long you will have weave poles and jumps, and maybe tunnels and contact obstacles, adorning your front or backyard—much to the amusement of your neighbors.

You should try *not* to have agility equipment set up where your dogs will play or run free during the day. Agility should be a supervised activity. Consider that you don't want your dog doing any of these things:

- Marking the equipment

- Chewing on the equipment

- Falling off/getting hurt on the equipment

- Taking obstacles because *he* decides to do so rather than being told to do an obstacle by you

- Getting bored with the equipment

- Learning that he can jump off contact obstacles without being released

Artist: Nancy Krouse-Culley

One of the first rules of agility is that it is a labor-intensive sport. So plan on putting away your equipment when it's not in use, or keep your equipment in a secured area.

Homework: *Come!*

For this exercise, get out that special food treat your dog would die for. Do *not* use a toy. You are going to teach your dog to *Come!* on command. This exercise is in three parts and is typically not something that you are going to accomplish in a day. Give yourself and your dog several days—or weeks if necessary—to master each part.

NOTE: There is no rule that says you must use *Come!* as the command to bring your dog to you. If you're afraid of confusing the agility *Come!* with a crisp obedience *Come!*, it is okay to use another word, such as *Here!*.

Part 1
1. Using a 10' to 12' lead, leave your dog on a stay and go out to the end of the lead and face the dog. Have your food treat in hand, ready for action.

2. Tell your dog to *Come!* in an enthusiastic voice.

3. If your dog does not immediately come to you, quickly reel him in to you using the lead.

4. Praise your dog enthusiastically and quickly give him the food treat.

When your dog consistently comes to you without an assist from the lead, proceed to Part 2.

Part 2
1. Leave your dog *off-lead* on a stay, and go out about 10' to 12' and face the dog. Have your food treat in hand, ready for action.

2. Tell your dog to *Come!* in an enthusiastic voice.

3. Praise your dog enthusiastically and quickly give him the food treat.

If your dog fails to come to you when called, you must return to Part 1 of this exercise. If your dog is consistently doing this exercise with enthusiasm, go on to Part 3.

Part 3

You will do the exercise as in Part 2. However, you should begin to:

- Increase the distance between you and your dog. Actually, you should vary the distance, one time doing the exercise from 20' and the next from 6'.

- Do the exercise from different places. Go behind the dog or off to the side of the dog. Go stand behind a tree or hide from view.

Four Poles

If you have been doing the exercises from the Student Notes, in Week 3 you began an exercise using two poles—sending your dog to enter the two poles (right-to-left), wrap around the second pole, and return to you. Now you are going to double the complexity of the exercise by adding two additional poles. To give the dog a bit of a break, you are going to tilt each pole 15° off center: odd poles to the left and even poles to the right.

At first, it may be necessary to move with your dog in order to pattern the movement through the poles. But, as soon as possible, you are going to make this a distance exercise by backing off until you never are closer than 10' to the dog or the line of poles.

After the dog has worked an entire week with no refusals or missed poles, you can gradually begin to raise the poles to an upright position.

Don't be in a big hurry. This exercise will pay really big dividends in the long run.

Favorite Motivator

Have you noticed your instructors talking about your dog's *favorite motivator*? This could be a food treat or a toy, such as a ball or Frisbee™.

In class, you should be using the *favorite* of your dog. Do you know which is your dog's favorite? If not, try asking your dog. Get your dog's favorite treat in one hand and his favorite toy in the other. Now, give him his choice. He will answer the question of favorites for you.

NOTE: On contact obstacles you should always use food. A toy motivator often encourages the dog to bail off the contact early. This would be detrimental to your training program in the long run.

A dog's favorite motivator will change from time to time. For example, the dog may be really hot for liver treats this week and only so-so care about them a few weeks later. With food it's sometimes useful to rotate what you use. Here are some ideas for you to try with your finicky eaters or for dogs that don't appear to be food motivated with run-of-the-mill treats:

- Roll-Over™ or Oinkeroll™
- Microwaved hot dog pieces
- Liver muffins (see the recipe from the Week 3 Student Notes)
- Beef processed in a food dehydrator at home
- Beefeaters Turkey Stix™
- Freeze-dried liver
- Easy Cheese™ or string cheese
- Tidbits of roastbeef or ham

Week 6: Instructor Notes

What do you do with a handler who blathers continuously while working his dog? Answer: Cookies. Stuff a handful of cookies in the handler's mouth and ask him, since he's in no position to talk back, to run a sequence of obstacles with his dog without saying *anything*. By doing this, most handlers quickly learn that it usually isn't the number or volume of words that communicates course flow to a dog.

Other handlers will add volume, or raise the voice an octave or two, or clap their hands only in competition. This very handler will explain to you that their dog performs perfectly in practice but *shuts down* in competition. It's too bad that handler can't compete with cookies in his mouth.

Artist: Nancy Krouse-Culley

	Jumps	Contacts	Poles/Table	Tunnels
Week 6	Review bar jump. Winged jumps. 6" for little dogs; 12" for big dogs. Review tire. Little dogs tire on ground; big dogs 12". Review long jump. Little dogs: two planks, 20"; big dogs: three planks, 30". Use bar jumps between planks.	Review dogwalk at 3'. Review A-frame at 4-1/2'. Review see-saw, gradually introducing plank movement.	Review weave poles with poles leaning 35° off center. Review table. Little dogs 6"; big dogs 12".	Review pipe tunnel in "U" shape. Review collapsed tunnel with 8' chute.

Organizational Notes

Review the Progress Worksheets from Week 5. Identify for your instructors those dogs most likely to have trouble with individual obstacles. If necessary, group together dogs having problems with specific obstacles.

Start the training session by doing the control exercise on page 79 with everyone. Then break into groups for the training sets, if you're going to work multiple sets simultaneously. Your working sets for this week are:

1. Weave pole sequence and see-saw review

2. Change of direction jumps

3. Snookered (a game)

4. Contact review sequences

Week 6: Progress Worksheet

Instructors: **Date:**

Handler and Dog	Attendance	Dogwalk	A-Frame	See-Saw	Weave Poles	Pipe Tunnel	Collapsed Tunnel	Bar Jump	Long Jump	Tire Jump	Table

GENERAL NOTES:

Week 6: Facility Layout

One square = 10'

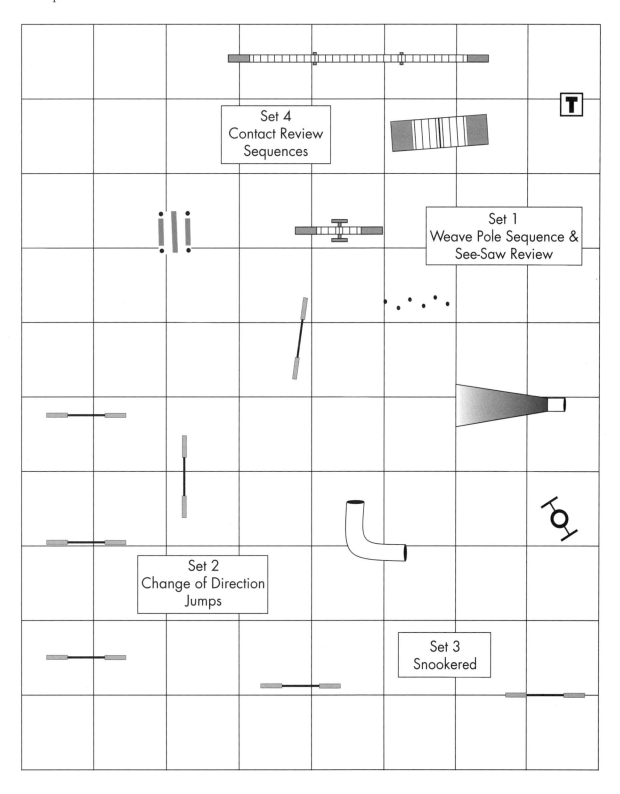

Set 4
Contact Review
Sequences

Set 1
Weave Pole Sequence &
See-Saw Review

Set 2
Change of Direction
Jumps

Set 3
Snookered

T

Week 6: Facility Layout Worksheet

Design your Facility Layout using a 1" = 10' scale (standard agility template)

WEEK 6

Week 6: Exercises

Start the class by doing the control exercise with everyone. Then break into smaller groups if you're going to work the training sets simultaneously.

Control Exercise

- Have your students free heel their dogs into the field of equipment. Don't work in a line—allow them to go where they will. Allow the dogs to sniff and to inspect the equipment, but keep the dogs off the equipment.

- Heel the dogs at attention into a long line. You need 8' to 10' between the dogs.

- *Down!* the dogs. Instruct handlers to leave their dogs and walk about 40', forming a line facing the dogs.

- Wait about two minutes (the instructor should keep time). If any dog breaks its stay during this time, the handler will collect the dog and hold on to it for the remainder of the exercise.

- Recall the dogs *one* at a time. Each handler commands his dog to *Come!* With any luck, the right dog will get up and come directly to the handler. If the dog does not, the handler will go and collect his dog. If the wrong dog comes, that dog's handler will collect his dog and put him back with the other dogs waiting to be recalled.

End of exercise. If any dogs are *not* coming to the handler, remind those handlers to continue working on their *Come!* command at home using a long line, food, and praise.

Set 1: Weave Pole Sequence and See-Saw Review

Your set consists of the weave poles, a bar jump, the see-saw, and the long jump. You will review each of the obstacles individually and then work on an obstacle sequence that includes the weave poles.

Review Weave Poles

Use a chute of six poles set up in a leaning poles configuration—first pole leans left, second pole leans right, and so forth, down the line. The poles are leaned 35° off center. Continue to use a bait plate at the end of the poles as you did in Week 5. The instructor should be the baitmaster. Dogs will be *off-lead* for this exercise.

1. With the dog on the handler's left, trot each dog down the chute of poles. If the dog cuts out, he should be put *back* on-lead for one or two repetitions.

2. Repeat step 1 with the dog working on the handler's right. If the dog cuts out he should be put *back* on-lead for one or two repetitions.

3. Repeat steps 1 and 2 until all dogs are comfortable.

Weave Poles to Bar Jump Sequence

Set a bar jump about 15' from the end of the weave poles. The jump should be set at 6" for little dogs and 12" for big dogs. This exercise should be performed *off-lead*.

1. With the dog on his left, have each handler take his dog through the weave poles.

2. Instruct your students that *as soon* as the dog's nose comes around the last pole, he should push towards the bar jump and give his dog the command to *Jump!*

3. After the dog is over the jump, the handler should praise, treat, and release.

Set 1
Weave Pole &
See-Saw Review

Review See-Saw

These instructions are based on the training program, "Walking the Plank: The Teeter", which is included in its entirety on pages 116–123. The instructions below are a summary of Phase 3 and Phase 4 of the program. The dog should be wearing a buckle collar and a short tab for this exercise. A spotter on the side opposite the handler may be useful to steady the dog and increase its sense of security. A second spotter will control the movement of the plank from *behind* the dog.

1. Place a food reward on the bottom of the plank. The spotter pushes down on the Side A end of the plank until the Side B end of the plank is 6" off the ground. Then, lift the dog onto *the center of the plank*, facing towards the Side B end of the plank.

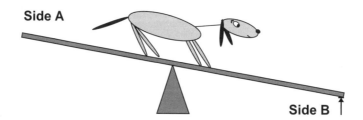

2. The spotter gently lowers the plank to the ground. The dog is praised and allowed to relax before proceeding.

3. Command the dog to *Walk!* and allow him to walk forward. The handler should signal to the waiting food to encourage the dog to focus downward to the end of the plank. Handlers should *not* use a verbal command like *Wait*—the dog is expected to stop at the end of the plank of his own volition. If the dog does so, he gets food. If he doesn't stop, pick up the dog and put him back on the plank.

4. The dog is not permitted to leave the plank until released with a quiet *Okay*. The exercise ends when the dog leaves the plank.

5. Repeat steps 1–4 until the dogs are calmly accepting the motion of the plank, focusing on the end of the plank, anticipating the food reward, and waiting for release before leaving the plank. Do not continue to step 6 until you have achieved this!

6. Repeat the entire exercise (steps 1–5) but this time have the spotter push down on the Side A end of the plank until the Side B end of the plank is 12" off the ground.

Review Long Jump

For little dogs, use a 6" jump between two long jump planks, with about a 20" spread. For big dogs, use two 12" bar jumps shuffled between three planks, with about a 30" spread. This exercise is performed *off-lead*.

Do two repetitions in this review:

1. Have the handler leave the dog in a sit-stay about 20' from the long jump. The handler takes up position about halfway to the long jump, to the right of the line the dog will take to the long jump. The handler should turn slightly and command his dog to *Come!* and then *Over!* Remind your students to get their hand (the one closest to the dog) out like a flag.

2. Have the handler leave the dog in a sit-stay about 20' from the long jump. Again the handler takes up position halfway to the long jump, but this time he stands to the left of the path that the dog will take to the jump. The handler again turns slightly and commands the dog to *Come!* and then *Over!*

3. Have the handler leave the dog in a sit-stay about 20' from the long jump. This time the handler moves to the far side of the long jump and commands the dog to *Come!* and then *Over!*

WEEK 6

Set 2: Change of Direction Jumps

The purpose of this *off-lead* exercise is to entice dogs to happily perform each jump in a continuous free-flowing sequence, while introducing a sudden change of direction. The jump height is *not* important; set the jumps at 6" for little dogs and 12" for big dogs.

Set 2
Change of Direction
Jumps

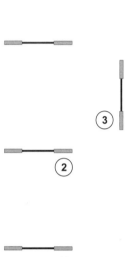

- For this exercise, make sure your students are armed with their dogs' favorite motivators, either food or a toy.

- Tell your students to use an unemotional *Wrong!* if the dog refuses a jump or takes the off-course jump. Don't give the reward and don't give praise. It's just wrong. *Allow the dogs to do the problem solving!* Be sure that the exercise ends on a positive note for each dog.

- If a dog skips a jump or takes the wrong course, just keep going. Do *not* attempt to circle back around on a jump to make a correction.

- Remind your students to use a hand signal and give a clear and early command to *Jump!* It's okay to repeat your command if your dog seems unfocused or uncertain.

- The handler should use a *Come!* command to change the direction of the dog's path towards him after jump #2. The handler should refrain from giving the dog a *Jump!* command for jump #3 until the dog actually turns towards that jump.

Set 3: Snookered (A Game!)

Start by reviewing each obstacle in this set individually: collapsed tunnel (with an 8' chute), pipe tunnel, and tire (set at ground level for little dogs and at 12" for big dogs). Perform the obstacle once with the dog working on the heel-side and then once with the dog on the off-side. Then, set up and play the game.

This is a quickie game that helps teach the rules of that ever popular agility game—Snooker.

Rules: Each dog and handler team has 30 seconds to earn as many points as possible. An off-course ends scoring.

1. A dog must take a jump labeled "Red". If successful, the dog earns one point and the right to do another obstacle for its point value (only one, and it cannot be another Red).

2. Do the other "Red" jump. If successful, the dog can do another extra obstacle.

3. Run the sequence #2 through #5.

HELPFUL HINT: The dog does not lose any points for faulting; a fault just results in ending the scoring. Consequently, it might be a good strategy to go out and get high-point obstacles in the opening sequence.

Set 4: Contact Review Sequences

Your set consists of the dogwalk and the A-frame, and the table. You will review each obstacle individually, as described below, and then combine the obstacles into short sequences.

Review Dogwalk

The dogwalk should be elevated to 2' or 3'. This exercise is performed *off-lead*.

1. Place a food reward on the lowest slat of the down-side contact zone.

2. With the dog on his left, the handler should command the dog to *Walk!* and allow him to ascend the plank. The handler should signal to the waiting food. If the dog stops at the end of the plank, he gets food. If he doesn't stop, pick up the dog and put him back on the plank at the point he left it.

3. Once the dog has paused, release him with a quiet *Okay*.

4. Repeat steps 1–3 once with the dog working on the handler's right.

Review A-Frame

Elevate the A-frame to 4-1/2'. You are going to introduce a handling maneuver. The exercise is performed *off-lead*.

1. Have the handler place a food treat on the lowest slat of the down-side contact zone. If possible, let the dog see the handler placing the treat.

2. With the dog on the handler's left, trot the dog up and over.

3. Allow the dog to get the food. Now, here comes the handling maneuver—as the dog is getting the treat, the handler will pivot in front of the dog, essentially to change sides to the dog while the dog is on the A-frame.

4. After the handler has changed sides, he should release the dog off the A-frame with a quiet *Okay*.

5. Repeat steps 1–4 once, working the dog on the handler's right.

NOTE: If the dog leaves the obstacle before being released, pick up the dog and place him back on the down ramp. Praise and release.

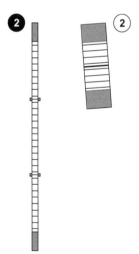

Review Table

Set the table to 6" for little dogs and 12" for big dogs. This exercise is performed *off-lead*.

1. The handler should place a food treat on the table.

2. The handler puts the dog up on the table and allows the dog to get the treat.

3. *Down!* the dog for a count of three seconds, then treat, release, and praise the dog.

4. Repeat steps 1–3. Handlers should hang back as their dog goes on to the table. If the dog won't advance beyond the handler, then the handler should immediately move in towards the table and put the dog up on the obstacle.

Table to Contact Sequence

After the obstacle reviews, set up the contact obstacles and table as shown in the illustration on the left.

Your students will alternately perform the A-frame and dogwalk, starting from the table each time.

Have each handler *Down!* his dog on the table, wait a short count (moving closer to the contact obstacle, if possible), and then call the dog to perform the obstacle.

Introductory Agility Workbook

Week 6: Student Notes

There are some noisy handlers out there. They talk too much. They talk too loudly. Sometimes they talk too harshly. Often they add other sounds to really set up an impressive din... clapping their hands, for instance. Handlers do this because they think their dogs understand all of the words they are saying. Some believe that it helps motivate their dogs.

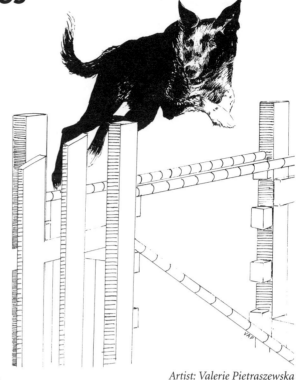

The motivation issue especially should be suspect. An under-motivated dog is frequently intimidated by his handler's antics rather than encouraged. It could be that an occasional well-timed "Good Dog" would sufficiently motivate a dog. But surely a constant and loud cacophony won't help much. Observe the dog's ears and tail as the handler unleashes the loud torrent of conversation. You will see many dogs flatten their ears and tuck their tails. This is body language that can be read like a book.

If you feel that your dog has a motivation problem, the next time you go to agility class, try working your dog without any verbal commands at all. Experiment. Try talking very quietly while you work your dog. See if the motivation problem improves at all.

Artist: Valerie Pietraszewska

Advanced Barrel Racing

In an earlier homework assignment, we had you teaching your dog to go out around two barrels, with you in the center. If your dog has been doing this exercise well, you're ready to take barrel training to the next level—you're going to add an obstacle.

1. Put a barrel on each side of a jump as shown in the illustration.

2. Standing in the middle by the jump, command the dog to *Jump!* and then send the dog out around the barrel.

3. As the dog comes around the barrel, call him back to you over the jump.

4. Repeat steps 2 and 3, sending the dog out around the other barrel.

This allows you to do a lot of work on your body positioning, without having to do a lot of running. The dog gets to do the running!

More Backyard Jumping

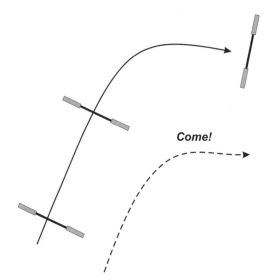

Come!

Use this simple sequence to polish your own handling skills. Some of your objectives include:

- Learn to use a hand signal. Use the hand closest to the dog (the hand on your left, for this exercise) to push out towards the jump, in a sawing motion. Keep the hand low enough to be in the dog's vision.

- Give a clear command to *Jump!*

- Give an early command to *Jump!* The timing of your command is very important. Don't wait for your dog's chin to be hanging over the bar of the next jump to give the command. You should be giving the command for the next jump while the dog is in the air over the previous jump. This kind of timing takes practice. Don't be impatient with yourself.

- Your dog may tend to run in a straight line. This means he will run out to the left of jump #2 or jump #3. This is important information for you because it will be your responsibility to change your dog's direction any time the course doesn't run in a straight line. Begin using *Come!* when you need to bend the dog's path towards you.

- Don't scold your dog. Don't hit your dog. Don't use loud and negative words with your dog when you are doing agility training. These are *not* good training techniques and will be counter-productive in the long run.

- Your job is to be a motivator and leader and partner for your dog. You will communicate to your dog from the onset that nothing in the whole world makes you happier than for him to briskly jump through this short sequence. You do this by giving enthusiastic praise at the completion of the exercise and offering the reward (food or toy).

- What you do when your dog does *not* do each jump is just as important as when he does. You should get it in your head quite early that you do *not* give an emotional or negative correction. Highly effective handlers will give the dog a neutral response. For instance, some handlers will say *Wrong!* in a flat and unemphatic voice. It's just *Wrong!* and you don't give the reward, and you don't give praise. It's just *Wrong!* Your dog is smart enough to figure out after a very short time that this flat and unassuming word usually means that no reward or praise is forthcoming. *Allow your dog to do the problem solving!*

Introductory Agility Workbook

WEEK 6

Week 7: Instructor Notes

When you have an outside teacher or seminar leader come to your club, it is both an interesting and an appalling process. It's good to watch your students learn fundamentals or advanced concepts from a master of the game. It's appalling to realize that your students will gush over the great stuff they learned and how their agility lives have been changed by the outside expert's observations—never mind that you've told them the *same* stuff a dozen or so times.

Outside experts are important, and even necessary. The instructor, to maintain his own dignity, must recognize certain immutable laws about experts and seminars:

- Experts are *always* from out of town—If the students know you, you can't be an expert.

- A seminar (8 to 16 hours on a weekend) allows *very focused* work. This focus is usually not possible in weekly classes, one hour at a time.

- In the end, your students will forget that you taught them the basics anyway.

Artist: Jo Ann Mather

But don't lose heart. When your students have progressed that far, then you really have done your job (and done it well!). Turn to the new crop of students coming up. Give them the same devotion. It's all worthwhile.

	Jumps	Contacts	Poles/Table	Tunnels
Week 7	Review bar jump. Winged and non-winged jumps. Little dogs 6"; big dogs 12". Review tire. Little dogs 6"; big dogs 12". Review long jump. Little dogs: two planks, 20"; big dogs: three planks, 30". Use bar jumps between planks.	Review dogwalk at 3'. Review A-frame at 4-1/2'. Review see-saw with dog beginning to initiate plank motion.	Review weave poles with poles leaning 35° off center. Review table. Little dogs 12"; big dogs 18".	Review pipe tunnel in "U" shape. Review collapsed tunnel with 12' chute.

Organizational Notes

Review the Progress Worksheets from Week 6. Identify for your instructors those dogs most likely to have trouble with individual obstacles. If necessary, group together dogs having problems with specific obstacles.

Start the training session by doing the control exercise on page 89 with everyone. Then break into groups for the training sets, if you're going to work multiple sets simultaneously. Your working sets for this week are:

1. Speed circle

2. Speed to table

3. Contact sequence and see-saw review

Week 7: Progress Worksheet

Instructors: Date:

Handler and Dog	Attendance	Dogwalk	A-Frame	See-Saw	Weave Poles	Pipe Tunnel	Collapsed Tunnel	Bar Jump	Long Jump	Tire Jump	Table

GENERAL NOTES:

Week 7: Facility Layout

One square = 10'

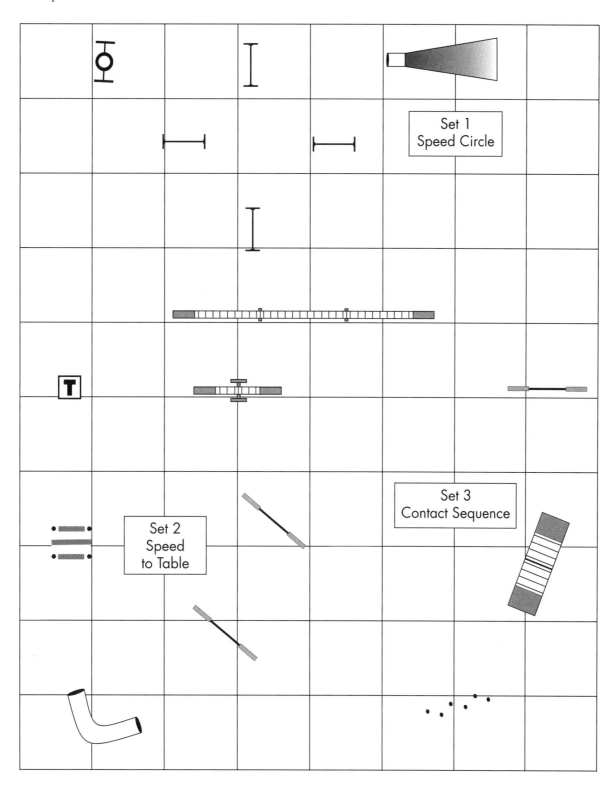

Set 1
Speed Circle

Set 3
Contact Sequence

Set 2
Speed
to Table

Week 7: Facility Layout Worksheet

Design your Facility Layout using a 1" = 10' scale (standard agility template)

Introductory Agility Workbook

WEEK 7

Week 7: Exercises

Start the class by doing the control exercise with everyone. Then break into smaller groups if you're going to work the training sets simultaneously. Since there are only three training sets this week and Set 3 contains a lot of obstacles to review, you should plan on giving each group extra time at that station.

Control Exercise

- Have your students free heel their dogs into the field of equipment. Don't work in a line—allow them to go where they will. Allow the dogs to sniff and to inspect the equipment, but keep the dogs off the equipment.

- Heel the dogs at attention into a long line. You need 8' to 10' between the dogs.

- *Down!* the dogs. Instruct handlers to leave their dogs and walk about 40', forming a line facing the dogs.

- Wait about two minutes (the instructor should keep time). If any dog breaks its stay during this time, the handler will collect the dog and hold on to it for the remainder of the exercise.

- Recall the dogs *one* at a time. Each handler commands his dog to *Come!* With any luck, the right dog will get up and come directly to the handler. If the dog does not, the handler will go and collect his dog. If the wrong dog comes, that dog's handler will collect his dog and put him back with the other dogs waiting to be recalled.

End of exercise.

Set 1: Speed Circle

Review both the collapsed tunnel (with a 12' chute) and the tire with your students before beginning the Speed Circle exercise. The tire and all of the bar jumps should be set to 6" for little dogs and 12" for big dogs.

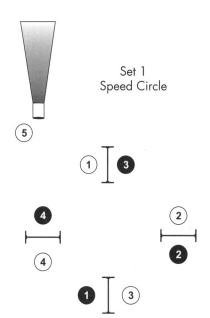

Set 1
Speed Circle

This is a slightly different look at the speed circle, but the basic objective stays the same.

- Starting at *white* jump #1, loop once through the circle, and out through the collapsed tunnel.

- Then, starting at *black* jump #1, loop once through the circle, and out through the tire.

This exercise is performed *off-lead*.

The *black* numbered sequence will give your students the most difficulty. In spite of the fact that you encourage as often as possible for them to work their dogs on either side, some of them will want to run with the dog in heel-side position.

Allow them to do so *once* without comment. That gives you a good basis to give them a small lecture on the efficiency of the handler taking the shorter inside path. That means that they have to learn to run with their dogs on their right, on the off-side. Do both sets again. This time, encourage the handlers to stay on the inside of the speed circle.

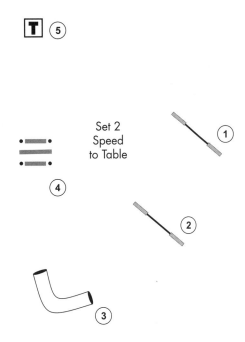

Set 2
Speed
to Table

Set 2: Speed to Table

The bar jumps should be set to 6" for little dogs and 12" for big dogs. With the long jump, for little dogs use a 6" jump between two long jump planks, with about a 20" spread; for big dogs, use two 12" bar jumps shuffled between three planks, with about a 30" spread. Set the table at 12" for little dogs and 18" for big dogs. This exercise is performed *off-lead*.

This kind of sequence is a test of control. The obvious problem is that a series of fast obstacles sets up an accelerated pace to the table. This may cause the dog to run by the table or to bounce on and off the obstacle.

What's the fix? Slow the handler down. If the handler slows, the dog will slow.

The presence of the long jump adds an additional challenge. You don't want to slow the dog to the extent that the dog shortens stride and faults the obstacle.

Set 3: Contact Sequence

Your set consists of the A-frame, a jump, a set of six weave poles, the dogwalk, and the see-saw. You will first review the contact obstacles and weave poles, and then combine all of the obstacles—with the exception of the see-saw—into a single sequence.

You must be on your guard to keep your students from hurrying over the obstacles. Some of them will be getting pretty cocky now and will want to feel the wind in their hair. It would be counter-productive for your students to fail to treat their dogs in the contact zones or to fail to require the dog to wait for a quiet release from the zones before continuing with the sequence.

Review Dogwalk

The dogwalk should be elevated to 2' or 3'. This exercise is performed *off-lead*.

1. Place a food reward on the lowest slat of the down-side contact zone.

2. With the dog on his left, the handler should command the dog to *Walk!* and allow him to ascend the plank. The handler should signal to the waiting food. If the dog stops at the end of the plank, he gets food. If he doesn't stop, pick up the dog and put him back on the plank at the point he left it.

3. Once the dog has paused, release him with a quiet *Okay*.

4. Repeat steps 1–3 once with the dog working on the handler's right.

Review A-Frame

Elevate the A-frame to 4-1/2'. The exercise is performed *off-lead*.

1. Have the handler place a food treat on the lowest slat of the down-side contact zone. If possible, let the dog see the handler placing the treat.

2. With the dog on the handler's left, trot the dog up and over.

3. The handler should allow the dog to get the food and then release the dog off the A-frame with a quiet *Okay*.

4. Repeat steps 1–3, working the dog on the handler's right.

NOTE: If the dog leaves the obstacle before being released, pick up the dog and place him back on the end of the down ramp. Praise and release.

WEEK 7

Review Weave Poles

Use a chute of six poles set up in a leaning poles configuration—first pole leans left, second pole leans right, and so forth, down the line. The poles are leaned 35° off center. You are going to allow a quick review only today. Dogs will be *off-lead* for this exercise.

1. With the dog on the handler's left, trot each dog down the chute of poles. If the dog cuts out, he should be put *back* on-lead for one or two repetitions.

That's all.

Review See-Saw

These instructions are based on the training program, "Walking the Plank: The Teeter", which is included in its entirety on pages 116–123. The instructions below are a summary of Phases 5 through 7 of the program. The dog should be wearing a buckle collar and a short tab. A spotter on the side opposite the handler may be useful to steady the dog. A second spotter will control the movement of the plank from *behind* the dog.

1. Place a food reward on the end of the plank. The spotter pushes down on the Side A end of the plank until the plank is parallel to the ground. Then, lift the dog onto *the center of the plank*, facing towards the Side B end.

    NOTE: Since most teeters are 24" high at the pivot point, you can ease the spotter's job by placing a 24" pause table under the end of the plank that the spotter is working. By pushing down on his end of the plank until it meets the table, the spotter can easily hold the plank steady as the dog is being placed on the center of the plank. Remember, the dog will be facing *away* from the table when he's placed on the plank.

2. The spotter gently lowers the plank to the ground. The dog is praised and allowed to relax before proceeding.

3. Command the dog to *Walk!* and allow him to walk forward. The handler should signal to the waiting food to encourage the dog to focus on the end of the plank. Handlers should *not* use a verbal command like *Wait*— the dog is expected to stop at the end of the plank of his own volition. If the dog does so, he gets food. If he doesn't stop, pick up the dog and put him back on the end of the plank.

4. The dog is not permitted to leave the plank until released with a quiet *Okay.*

5. Repeat steps 1–4 until the dogs are calmly accepting the motion of the plank, focusing on the end of the plank, anticipating the food reward, and waiting for release before leaving the plank. Do not continue to step 6 until you have achieved this!

6. Place a food reward on the end of the plank. The spotter pushes down on the Side A end of the plank until the plank is parallel to the ground. Then lift the dog onto *the Side A end of the plank*, facing towards the Side B end of the plank.

7. Command the dog to *Walk!* and allow him to walk forward. The handler should signal to the waiting food to encourage the dog to focus on the end of the plank. The spotter gently lowers the plank to the ground as the dog passes the pivot point. The dog is praised and allowed to relax before proceeding. The dog is *not* encouraged to come to a complete stop at the pivot point unless the motion of the teeter frightens him.

8. Encourage the dog to continue walking forward slowly. The handler should signal to the waiting food. The dog is expected to stop at the end of the plank of his own volition. If the dog does so, he gets food. If he doesn't stop, pick up the dog and put him back on the end of the plank.

9. The dog is not permitted to leave the plank until released with a quiet *Okay.*

10. Repeat steps 6–9 until the dogs are calmly accepting the motion of the plank. Then on subsequent repetitions, have the rear spotter start allowing *the dog* to lower the plank to the ground as the dog passes the pivot point. The spotter should, however, be prepared to move in and ease the plank to the ground, if the dog is going up the plank too quickly.

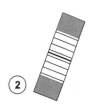

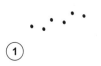

Weave to A-Frame Sequence

Dogs will be *off-lead* for this exercise.

- Handlers should briefly praise their dogs after the weave poles and then attack the A-frame.

- Be sure to continue using treats on the down-side contact of the A-frame.

- If the dog leaves the A-frame before being released by the handler, pick up the dog and place him back on the down ramp. Praise and release.

Encourage your students to try this exercise once beginning with the dog on the left; and then try it again beginning with the dog on the right. Your students may find that it is easier starting with the dog on their right.

Jump to Dogwalk Sequence

Demonstrate the following two handling positions for this exercise. Your students should try both.

- In the first instance, the handler will work on the left side of the jump. He will turn his body abruptly as the dog commits over the jump, give the dog the command to *Come!,* and when the dog's nose is turned pointing to the dogwalk, he will give the command to *Walk!*

- In the second instance, the handler will leave the dog in a sit-stay on one side of the jump and move to the far side of the jump. This puts the jump directly in the path of the dog as he comes to the handler. As the dog is committed to the jump, the handler will pivot abruptly right, give a clear hand signal, and command the dog to *Walk!*

In both instances the handler, or a baitmaster, should treat the down-side contact of the dogwalk prior to starting the exercise so that the dog is duly rewarded at the end of the plank. Remember that the dog is *not* allowed to leave the plank until released by the handler. If he does so, the dog should be picked up and placed back on the plank.

Dogs will be *off-lead* for this exercise.

WEEK 7

Week 7: Student Notes

What do *you* do when the raindrops start falling on your head during a training session? Pack it up, run for the van, cover the pooch... right?

You should know that dog agility is a lot like NFL football—it is played in any weather. Very few matches get called on account of rain (unless there's lightning) or even snow. Usually the show goes on.

If you are going to compete in wet weather, or cold slushy weather, you have to train in that kind of weather. So, next time it starts raining outside, don't call the dog in and light the fire. Instead, strap on the bait pouch, put on a sturdy hat and slicker, and take the dog out to play.

Keep it safe so that you aren't pitching your dog at slippery contacts at full speed. Jumps, a pipe tunnel, and the table should do nicely.

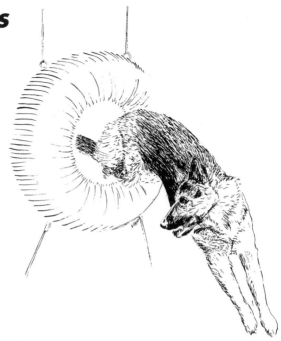

Artist: Valerie Pietraszewska

Weave Pole Chute

The goal of this exercise is a fast, enthusiastic run.

1. Run with your dog as you send him through the weave pole chute. Do several repetitions with the dog running on your left and several with the dog running on your right.

2. Leave your dog at one end of the poles and then go to the other end and call your dog through the chute.

3. Now you're going to work around the clock. Have a member of your household or a friend hold your dog at the entrance to the poles—the six o' clock position. You will move to different positions "around the clock" as shown in Figure 1 below. Call the dog through using a voice command and a good hand signal. Give immediate praise and reward as the dog comes through the poles. The entry must be perfect before going to next step.

4. Introduce an angled entry to the weave pole chute. This time the dog works around the clock, as shown in Figure 2 below, while the handler stays at the twelve o'clock position.

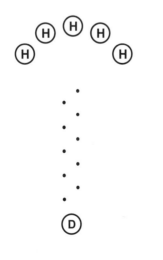

Figure 1

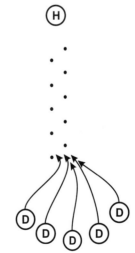

Figure 2

My Dog, My Jump, and Me

Here are a series of exercises suited to the backyard or the neighborhood park. Each exercise uses one or two jumps only; but the skills being added to your agility repertoire are of immense value to your long term success.

Use food treats in these exercises and happy praise. Failure to perform should *not* be punished by emotional correction—just withhold the treats and praise.

Don't be in too big of a hurry to progress through the exercises. Your dog should experience a 90% or better success rate. If you aren't being that successful it does *not* mean your dog isn't smart. It means you're moving too fast, and you are risking stressing the dog.

Remember to always end your practice sessions with success and on a positive note.

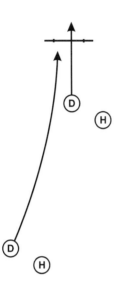

Send Away

Want to really impress your friends with a basic backyard agility trick? Try sending your dog the length of your back yard to jump.

1. Start very close to the jump. Initially, you may have to move with your dog (maybe even brush past the jump), to get your dog over the jump. As your dog begins to anticipate your command in order to get the praise and treat reward, you know you can begin to move further back.

2. Gradually increase the starting position between you, your dog, and the jump. *Gradually* means back up a half a step after three or four successful repetitions from the *same* spot. Don't be in too big of a hurry.

It's likely that when you go out to do this exercise, your dog won't immediately be ready to start at the longest distance you used in your last outing with the exercise. Plan on slowly graduating (increasing) your starting position for this exercise, over a period of weeks and months.

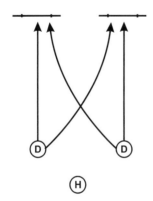

Send Away: Dog's Choice

Don't begin doing this exercise until you and your dog have mastered the basic send away to jump.

The chief difference in this exercise is that the dog has a choice in which jump to perform. Clearly your dog already knows how to jump and is motivated to do so. You must work on using a hand signal and body movement to communicate your choice of jumps to the dog.

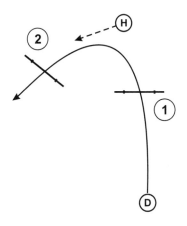

Double-Pump: To and Fro

This exercise combines the basic recall with the send away.

Call your dog over jump #1, and then immediately send the dog away over jump #2.

Also try putting the second jump on the other side of jump #1 so you can practice right turns as well as left.

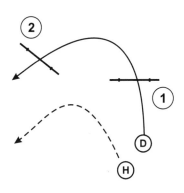

Double-Pump: Away and To

This is another combination exercise. Notice that some movement is required on your part. As much as possible you want to create a path for yourself that parallels the dog's path after the dog turns from performance of jump #1.

Also try putting the second jump on the other side of jump #1 so you can practice right turns as well as left.

Agility Jump Heights

The height that your dog must jump in agility competition is based on the dog's height at the withers (his shoulders). Each agility organization has different rules and different jump height requirements. As jump heights and equipment specifications change from time to time, it is a good idea to write to the organizations under which you may eventually compete and obtain a current rulebook. Addresses and phone numbers of these organizations are listed on the Agility Resource Sheet that is available from your instructor.

United States Dog Agility Association (USDAA)

Jump Height	Dog's Height
12"	12" and under
18"	16" and under but over 12"
24"	21" and under but over 16"
30"	Over 21"

American Kennel Club (AKC)

Jump Height	Dog's Height
8"	10" and under
12"	14" and under but over 10"
16"	18" and under but over 14"
20"	22" and under but over 18"
24"	Over 22"

NADAC (North American Dog Agility Council (NADAC)

Jump Height	Dog's Height
8"	10" and under
12"	12" and under but over 10"
16"	16" and under but over 12"
20"	20" and under but over 16"
24"	Over 20"

Australian Shepherd Club of America (ASCA)

Jump Height	Dog's Height
8"	10" and under
12"	12" and under but over 10"
16"	16" and under but over 12"
20"	20" and under but over 16"
24"	Over 20"

United Kennel Club (UKC)

Jump Height	Dog's Height
8"	14" and under
14"	20" and under but over 14"
20"	Over 20"

Agility Association of Canada (AAC)

Jump Height	Dog's Height
12"	12" and under
18"	16" and under but over 12"
24"	21" and under but over 16"
30"	Over 21"

Week 8: Instructor Notes

It is your trained eye that must assess a dog's fitness for agility training. The dog's age, weight, and soundness must be taken into consideration. You should counsel the owner of an unfit dog. Usually, reduced obstacle heights can accommodate most dogs; but in the most exaggerated cases, you might have to deny a dog's participation in class.

An overweight dog is prone to injury and will often have a problem with agility. A weight that is fine in the breed ring is probably too darned fat for agility.

Here are a couple of simple tests: Can you easily feel the dog's ribs? When you look down at the dog, does it have an hourglass figure? (You should be able to see where the dog's waist actually begins.) When you look at the dog from the side, does the dog's stomach "tuck up"?

Artist: Karen Gaydos

Important Qualities of a Good Teacher
One of the most important qualities of a good teacher is humor. Many are the purposes it serves. The most obvious one is that it keeps the pupils alive and attentive because they are never quite sure what is coming next. Another is that it does in fact help to give a true picture of many important subjects.

—Gilbert Highet, *The Art of Teaching*

	Jumps	Contacts	Poles/Table	Tunnels
Week 8	Review bar jump. Winged and non-winged jumps. Little dogs 6"; big dogs 12". Review tire. Little dogs 6"; big dogs 12". Review long jump. Little dogs: two planks, 20"; big dogs: three planks, 30". Use bar jumps between planks.	Review dogwalk at 3'. Review A-frame at 4-1/2'. Review see-saw starting dogs from the ground.	Review weave poles with poles leaning 30° off center. Review table. Little dogs 12"; big dogs 18".	Review pipe tunnel in "U" shape. Review collapsed tunnel with 12' chute.

Organizational Notes

Congratulations on having survived to the final class of the Introductory Agility program! Today the format of class has been altered to test how your students are doing in a fun way. You will briefly review the table, weave poles, and see-saw, and then you will have your students run the graduation course.

This lesson plan is written so that you can take your entire class around the course in a walk-through and look at the different segments of the course. You should plan on allowing two or three dogs to demonstrate the handling challenges of each segment. You could further modify this by breaking up into sets, which you will quickly rotate, to allow everyone at least one good look at each of the segments. But, allow yourself enough time to actually run the graduation course (which is a pairs relay) at least once, and hopefully twice.

Speed is *not* the objective of the graduation course, but you can bet some of your competitive students will want it to be a race. Consequently, we've built into the plan the *requirement* that dogs get a treat on all contacts.

Don't forget to give diplomas to your human students, and biscuits or special treats to your canine students!

Week 8: Progress Worksheet

Instructors: Date:

Handler and Dog	Attendance	Dogwalk	A-Frame	See-Saw	Weave Poles	Pipe Tunnel	Collapsed Tunnel	Bar Jump	Long Jump	Tire Jump	Table

GENERAL NOTES:

WEEK 8

Week 8: Facility Layout

One square = 10'

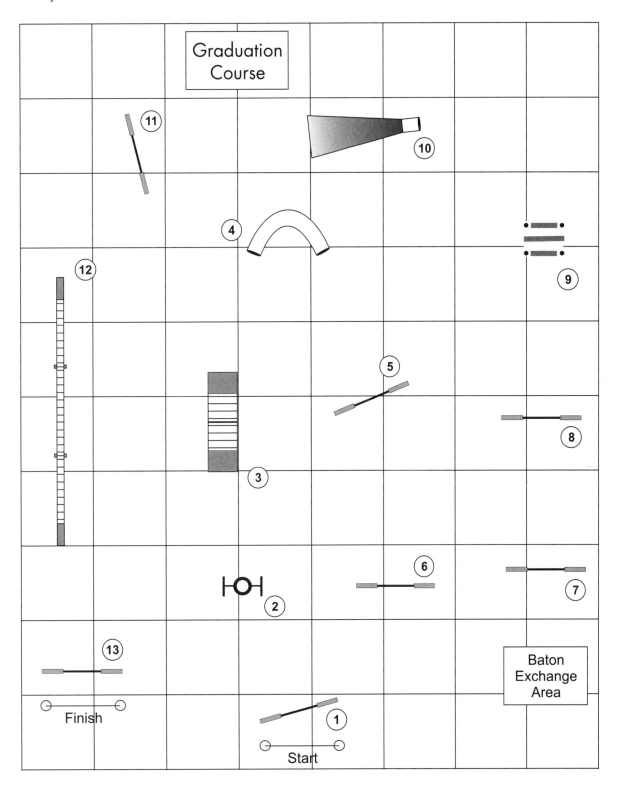

Graduation Course

Baton Exchange Area

Finish

Start

Week 8: Facility Layout Worksheet

Design your Facility Layout using a 1" = 10' scale (standard agility template)

Week 8: Exercises

The exercises this week are break-down exercises; that is, each sequence is part of a larger course. After briefly trying each set (or just demonstrating the set with several dogs), the class will run the graduation course.

Weave Pole and Table Review

You are going to allow only a quick review of the weave poles and table today; neither obstacle is used in the graduation course. Use a chute of six poles set up in a leaning poles configuration—first pole leans left, second pole leans right, and so forth, down the line. The poles are leaned 30° off center. Set the table at 12" for little dogs and 18" for big dogs. Dogs will be *off-lead* for this exercise.

- With the dog on the handler's left, trot each dog down the chute of poles.

- Have each handler approach the table with his dog, command the dog up on the table, and put the dog in a down position. Quickly give the dog a treat on the table and release.

That's all.

See-Saw Review

These instructions are based on the training program, "Walking the Plank: The Teeter", which is included in its entirety on pages 116–123. The instructions below are a summary of Phase 8 of the program. The dog should be wearing a buckle collar and a short tab. A spotter on the side opposite the handler may be useful to steady the dog. A second spotter should be ready to come in *behind* the dog and gently lower the plank to the ground as the dog passes the pivot point, *if necessary* (for example, if the dog is running up the plank too quickly).

1. Place a treat on the Side A end of the plank. Start the dog *from the ground* at the Side B end of the plank.

2. Command the dog to *Walk!* and allow him to walk forward. The handler should signal to the waiting food to encourage the dog to focus on the end of the plank. The spotter should allow *the dog* to lower the plank to the ground as he passes the pivot point. The dog is praised and allowed to relax before proceeding. Do *not* encourage the dog to come to a complete stop at the pivot point unless the motion of the teeter frightens him.

3. The handler should encourage the dog to continue walking forward slowly and signal to the waiting food. The handler should not use a verbal command like *Wait*—the dog is expected to stop at the end of the plank of his own volition. If the dog does so, he gets food. If he doesn't stop, pick up the dog and put him back on the end of the plank.

4. The dog is not permitted to leave the plank until released with a quiet *Okay*. The dog should not associate leaving the plank with positive reinforcement—positive reinforcement should occur only in the contact zone. The exercise ends when the dog leaves the plank.

5. Repeat steps 1–4 until the dogs are calmly initiating and accepting the motion of the plank, focusing on the end of the plank, anticipating the food reward, and waiting for release before leaving the plank.

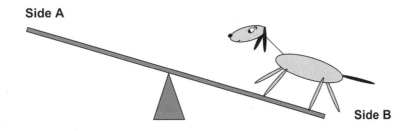

Side A

Side B

Graduation Course

This is a game and should be made as fun as possible for your students. Tell everyone to cheer enthusiastically for each other as they complete the course. Use the course depicted on the Facility Worksheet on page 99.

Briefing

- This is a relay course. We'll divide the class into teams of two dogs and two handlers each. The first dog and handler on each team will run obstacles #1 through# 6. The second dog and handler on the team will run obstacles #7 through #13.

- The first handler on the course will carry a baton over the first part of the course then hand the baton off to the second handler.

- There are two contact obstacles in this course. The handler on the course is *required* to have a treat ready for the dog in the down-side contact zone of the obstacle. The dog should not be allowed to leave the obstacle until the handler has given a quiet release. This means that each handler must have a treat ready.

- There will be no weave poles or table or see-saw on this course.

- The team with the fastest time wins.

- After everyone has run the course, each team will switch sides of the course and run it again. This way everyone will get a chance to run both parts of the course.

Walking the Course

In competition, all exhibitors are allowed to walk the course prior to running the course with their dogs; however, they may not take their dogs with them. This isn't really competition though…we're in training. So, everyone will get to take their dogs with them while we walk the course first as a class. We will look at four different elements of the pairs course. You will have some dogs run each of the course segments to illustrate the handling possibilities. If you have a really big class, you need to make sure that you give everybody at least one opportunity to be a demo dog; but don't use up class time having every dog work every segment.

Walking a course is the handler's opportunity to first of all figure out what the sequence of the course is, and then to commit it to memory. It also allows the handler to work out what commands he will use, how he will move his body, and how to negotiate any traps (often called handler challenges) in the course. In a pairs course, which is what this is, each member of the team will also figure out which side of the course they will run and will even practice handing off the baton in the baton exchange area.

③

②

①

Start

Opening Sequence

- In the opening sequence, a flow is set up that builds some speed to the A-frame. Many dogs having trouble with the tire may refuse the obstacle, electing to run around it, rather than jump through it.

- For the tire, on the first pass, the handler should give a very clear hand signal to the dog, directing the dog to jump the tire. It would be useful for the handler to lead out somewhat to be in position to give a good hand signal.

- If the dog initially refuses the tire, advise your students to plan on quickly putting the dog back on the right side of the tire in a sit-stay, go around to the other side and call the dog through. Remind them to get right up in the opening of the tire so that the hoop frames the handler's head and arms.

- Remind your students to have a treat ready for the A-frame. They will be *required* to give the dog a treat in the down contact zone when doing the A-frame (it's not optional).

④

⑤

⑥

Tunnel Turnaround

In this sequence, the handler will stick the dog into the tunnel and then race the dog past the two remaining jumps. This is a simple sequence complicated only by the fact that the handler has to all at once get control of his dog after the final jump, and hand the baton off to the second handler.

As a matter of strategy, racing the dog could allow the handler to get down and hand off the baton ahead of the dog. The dog might even move faster, seeing his handler running away. On the down side, the dog might run around one or both of the jumps, forcing the handler to go back and fix the missed jumps.

Remind your students to give a good hand signal and voice command for each of the obstacles in this sequence.

After handing off the baton, the handler should get control of his dog and hold onto the dog while the second handler runs his dog over the second sequence of obstacles.

(10)

(9)

Second Dog's Opening

After receiving the baton, the second dog and handler may start. They *must* receive the baton in the baton exchange area. What does this mean? It means that there is no opportunity for the second handler to lead out from the dog.

The second dog and handler are initially faced with a series of three jumps and then an abrupt turn to the left. This means that the handler will start with his dog (or should start with his dog) on his right side.

The key to the opening series of jumps is for the handler to run good and fast. As *soon* as the dog is committed over the long jump, the handler needs to make an abrupt turn to the left, using the *Come!* command to turn the dog, before instructing the dog to get in the tunnel.

(8)

(7)

(11)

The Closing Sequence

The closing sequence is especially challenging because it sets up a lot of speed for the dog, and requires the dog to suddenly be under control as he ascends the dogwalk.

Remind your students to have a treat ready because they will be *required* to give the dog a treat in the down-side contact zone. The dog should remain in the contact zone until the handler gives a quiet release.

(12)

(13)

Finish

WEEK 8

Week 8: Student Notes

Sportsmanship is grace and humor, in equal portions. It's about how we handle losing, and how we handle winning. I'm not too sure that either grace or humor can be taught.

The first sign of a poor sport is assigning blame to anyone/ anything besides one's self. It was my partner's fault; it was the gate steward's fault; it was the judge's fault; it was my dog's fault.

It's relatively easy to take responsibility for what happens in the agility ring. That's all it takes. Admit it. Face it. It was probably your fault. As soon as you realize this you can put a smile back on your face and get on with the day.

A judge might not fault a handler for fits of bad temper unless the blame is directed to the dog. It's almost never the dog's fault. And, even if it were...so what?

Artist: Nancy Krouse-Culley

Squaring Up

There are times when the approach to a contact obstacle is at such an angle that the dog has to make a special effort to square up for the ascent in order to avoid getting on the side of the ramp and missing the contact.

You can teach the dog to square up for the obstacle by "gating" the up ramp of the obstacle. Gates can be made from hoops, traffic cones, baby gates, sections of the long jump, driveway markers or poles that stick in the ground, and so on. The idea is to create a physical "channel" that will encourage the dog to straighten out his approach to the obstacle without intervention from the handler.

Consistency on the part of the handler is the key to the dog understanding the job. You treat, reward, and praise your dog for squaring up for the gates and getting on the obstacle straight. You withhold treats, rewards, and praise for failing to square up for the gates.

Start by sending your dog to the obstacle from an easy angle and then progressively increase the difficulty of the approach. Proof your dog by removing the gates from the obstacle. Does the dog square up for the obstacle as though the gates were in place? If so, the dog has learned the job. There are times when an approach to a contact obstacle is at such an angle that the dog will have to make a special effort to square up for the ascent in order to avoid the missed contact fault.

Teach the dog to square up for the obstacle by "gating" it. Gates can be made from hoops, traffic cones, baby gates, or weave poles. Over time, set up exercises which create a variety of approaches to the contact obstacle.

Homework: *Side!*

Besides having a *Heel!* command to instruct your dog to be on your left side, in agility it's very useful to have a *Side!* command to instruct your dog to move to your right side.

Sometimes it's a good idea to return to obedience basics to teach a new concept. The way you taught *Heel!* in the first place was to shape a behavior—you put a name to a specific action and then you rewarded that action.

Teaching a dog to move to your right side can be taught in the same way that you taught the dog to move to your left side—a dog will quickly learn to equate moving to your right side when you say *Side!* to earning a treat.

Clean Run Magazine

This workbook was designed for you by the editors of the *Clean Run*, a monthly agility magazine for those who have been seriously bitten by the agility bug. For a sample copy of the *Clean Run* send $6.00 to Clean Run Productions at 35 Walnut Street, Turners Falls, MA 01376-2317 or (call 413) 863-8303.

WEEK 8

Your next Clean Run is only as far away as your mailbox!

- Articles by top agility competitors in the U.S. and abroad

- Training exercises for all levels

- Courses and course analyses

- Discussions of rules by judges

- Handling strategies

- Discussions of training problems

- Teaching ideas and plans for instructors

- Changes and trends in USDAA®, AKC®, and NADAC agility

☐ I want to sign up for a year of the *Clean Run* and am enclosing $60 ($66 Canada or $85 Overseas).

☐ Please rush me a sample copy of *Clean Run* magazine for $6.

☐ **VISA**   ☐ MasterCard   ☐ Check or money order (US funds)

TOTAL ENCLOSED: $_____

☐☐☐☐☐ ☐☐☐☐☐ ☐☐☐☐☐ ☐☐☐☐☐

Expiration Date: ☐☐ ☐☐

Signature: _____
(Charge not valid unless signed)

Name (Please print clearly): _____

Company or Group: _____

Mailing Address: _____

City: _____   State/Prov: _____   Zip+4 Code: _____

Country: _____   E-Mail: _____

Mail orders to Clean Run Productions
35 Walnut Street, Turners Falls, MA 01376-2317
Or order by phone: (413) 863-8303

Appendix

Training the Dogwalk

Training the A-Frame

Training the See-Saw

Training the Weave Poles

A Philosophy for Training to Win

Dog Profile Form

Agility Resource Sheet

Training Methodology Q&A

Artist: Bud Houston

Training the Dogwalk

The desired performance of the dog walk can be described as follows:

• The dog ascends the obstacle in the direction indicated by the course flow.

• The dog must touch the yellow contact zone on the ascent.

• The dog must touch the yellow contact zone on the descent.

Performances that are faulted include:

Refusal A dog is deemed to have refused the dogwalk in several circumstances:

• If the dog crosses the run-out planes defined for the obstacle. The plane for the dogwalk is the back edge of the contact zone on the ascent ramp. If the dog has to back up or turn around to ascend the plank, it is a refusal.

• If the dog commits to the obstacle and gets back off before starting descent.

• If the dog advances towards the obstacle, focuses on the obstacles, and turns back. It's possible that a handler could cause this fault by calling the dog away from the dogwalk after the dog has clearly committed towards it.

Missed Contact A missed contact is incurred when the dog fails to touch either the ascent side or descent side contact zones. These are usually painted yellow. In some agility organizations (such as NADAC), it is not considered a fault to miss the ascent side contact zone. However, it is certainly a mistake not to train the dog to always hit the up-side contact.

Failure to Perform Failure to perform is earned when the dog omits the dogwalk.

Off-Course An off-course is incurred when a dog performs the dogwalk in the wrong direction; that is, in a direction other than the one determined by the judge.

Safety Rule In the USDAA Starters level, and at all levels of AKC competition, if the dog commits to the dogwalk with all four paws and then jumps off, the dog and handler are required to skip the obstacle and continue with the course. They will earn a failure to perform fault for this omission. If the dog is allowed to get back on the obstacle by his handler, the dog and handler will be immediately excused from the ring.

Walking the Plank: The Dogwalk

by Linda Mecklenburg

Success in teaching or retraining the dogwalk and getting a fast, accurate performance from your dog, rests in your patience and ability to be consistent in the application of positive and negative reinforcement. This training program consists of 12 phases and relies on two fundamental rules:

1. The dog is rewarded with food treats and praise for being in the contact zone.

2. The dog is corrected for leaving the contact zone (simply by picking up the dog and putting him back on the end of the plank) without a command from the handler.

The desired outcome of this program is a dog that races up and over the dogwalk. The dog pauses imperceptibly in the contact zone and then proceeds ahead on course as directed.

NOTE: A low dogwalk is helpful for this training program.

Phase 1: First Contact

The dog should be wearing a buckle collar and a short tab for this phase of training. The collar and tab allow you to control the dog on the plank. Have a food reward ready in hand.

1. Lift the dog onto *the end of the down plank*, facing off the dogwalk, and reward him with food and praise for remaining there. The dog can be in any position but standing is preferred. At first the food is given directly to the dog; then it is placed on the end of the plank. Your task is to signal to the food by pointing to it with the hand closest to the dog and touching it, encouraging the dog to focus downward to the end of the plank.

2. If the dog attempts to leave the plank, pick up the dog and put him back on the plank. Then reward the dog again for being in the contact zone.

3. The dog is not permitted to leave the plank until you release him with a quiet *Okay*. Do not praise the dog or celebrate as the dog leaves the plank. Do not use food or toys as the dog leaves the plank. *You do not want the dog to associate leaving the plank with positive reinforcement—positive reinforcement should occur only in the contact zone.* Do not send the dog to another obstacle. The exercise ends when the dog leaves the plank. You may restart the exercise.

Do not continue to Phase 2 unless the dog is focusing on the end of the plank, anticipating the food reward, and waiting for release before leaving the plank.

Phase 2: Midway on the Down Plank

The dog should be wearing a buckle collar and a short tab. Have a food reward waiting on the end of the plank.

1. Lift the dog onto the *center of the down plank*.

2. Command the dog to *Walk!* and then guide him forward. Signal to the waiting food to encourage the dog to focus downward to the end of the plank. Do *not* use a verbal command like *Wait*—the dog is expected to stop at the end of the plank of his own volition. If the dog does so, he gets food. If the dog doesn't stop, pick up the dog and put him back on the plank.

3. The dog is not permitted to leave the plank until released. In this phase, use only a quiet *Okay* to release the dog. Don't give the dog food or use a toy. Don't ask the dog to do additional obstacles. *All positive reinforcement should occur in the contact zone.*

Do not continue to Phase 3 unless the dog is focusing on the end of the plank, anticipating the food reward, and waiting for release before leaving the plank.

Phase 3: Top of the Down Plank

The dog should be wearing a buckle collar and a short tab. Have a food reward waiting at the end of the plank.

1. Lift the dog onto the *top of the down plank*.

2. Command the dog to *Walk!* and allow him to walk forward. Signal to the waiting food to encourage the dog to focus downward to the end of the plank. Do *not* use a verbal command like *Wait*—the dog is expected to stop at the end of the plank of his own volition. If the dog does so, he gets food. If the dog doesn't stop, pick up the dog and put him back on the plank.

3. The dog is not permitted to leave the plank until released. In this phase, use only a quiet *Okay* to release the dog. Don't give the dog food or use a toy. Don't ask the dog to do additional obstacles. *All positive reinforcement should occur in the contact zone.*

Do not continue to Phase 4 unless the dog is focusing on the end of the plank, anticipating the food reward, and waiting for release before leaving the plank.

Phase 4: Back It Up to the Center Plank

The dog should be wearing a buckle collar and a short tab. Have a food reward waiting on the end of the plank.

1. Lift the dog onto the *middle of the center plank.*

2. Command the dog to *Walk!* and allow him to walk forward. Signal to the waiting food to encourage the dog to focus downward to the end of the plank. Do *not* use a verbal command like *Wait*—the dog is expected to stop at the end of the plank of his own volition. If the dog does so, he gets food. If the dog doesn't stop, pick up the dog and put him back on the plank.

3. The dog is not permitted to leave the plank until released. In this phase, use only a quiet *Okay* to release the dog. Don't give the dog food or use a toy. Don't ask the dog to do additional obstacles. *All positive reinforcement should occur in the contact zone.*

Do not continue to Phase 5 unless the dog is focusing on the end of the plank, anticipating the food reward, and waiting for release before leaving the plank.

Phase 5: The Up Plank (At Last!)

The dog should be wearing a 6' lead for this phase of training. The lead allows you to promptly correct the dog should he fail to stop for the food reward which should be waiting at the end of the plank.

1. Start the dog *from the ground.*

2. Command the dog to *Walk!* and allow him to ascend the plank at any speed. Signal to the waiting food to encourage the dog to focus downward to the end of the plank. Do *not* use a verbal command like *Wait*—the dog is expected to stop at the end of the plank of his own volition. If the dog does so, he gets food. If the dog doesn't stop, pick up the dog and put him back on the plank.

3. The dog is not permitted to leave the plank until released. In this phase, use only a quiet *Okay* to release the dog. Don't give the dog food or use a toy. Don't ask the dog to do additional obstacles. *All positive reinforcement should occur in the contact zone.*

Do not continue to Phase 6 unless the dog is focusing on the end of the plank, anticipating the food reward, and waiting for release before leaving the plank.

Phase 6: Off-Lead

The dog should be off-lead for the first time. Have a food reward waiting on the end of the plank.

1. Start the dog *from the ground.*

2. Command the dog to *Walk!* and allow him to ascend the plank. Signal to the waiting food to encourage the dog to focus downward to the end of the plank. Do *not* use a verbal command like *Wait*—the dog is expected to stop at the end of the plank of his own volition. If the dog does so, he gets food. If the dog doesn't stop, pick up the dog and put him back on the plank.

3. The dog is not permitted to leave the plank until released. In this phase, use only a quiet *Okay* to release the dog. Don't give the dog food or use a toy. Don't ask the dog to do additional obstacles. *All positive reinforcement should occur in the contact zone.*

Do not continue to Phase 7 unless the dog is focusing on the end of the plank, anticipating the food reward, and waiting for release before leaving the plank.

Phase 7: Food In Hand

The dog should be off-lead. Have the food reward in hand, rather than leaving it at the end of the down plank.

1. Start the dog *from the ground.*

2. Command the dog to *Walk!* and allow him to ascend the plank. Signal to the end of the down plank with your inside hand (the hand closest to the dog), actually touching the end of the down plank. As the dog approaches the zone, *wait for the dog to pause,* and then *immediately* place the food on the end of the plank. Carry the food in your outside hand; that is, the hand farthest away from the dog and the dogwalk. Do *not* use a verbal command like *Wait*—the dog is expected to stop at the end of the plank of his own volition. If the dog does so, he gets food. If the dog doesn't stop, pick up the dog and put him back on the plank.

3. The dog is not permitted to leave the plank until released. In this phase, use only a quiet *Okay* to release the dog. Don't give the dog food or use a toy. Don't ask the dog to do additional obstacles. *All positive reinforcement should occur in the contact zone.*

Do not continue to Phase 8 unless the dog is focusing on the end of the plank, anticipating the food reward, and waiting for release before leaving the plank.

Phase 8: Increased Time and Distance

The dog should be off-lead. Have the food reward in hand, rather than leaving it at the end of the down plank.

1. Start the dog *from the ground.*

2. Command the dog to *Walk!* and allow him to ascend the plank. Signal to the end of the down plank to encourage the dog to focus downward. As the dog approaches the zone, wait for the dog to pause, and then place the food reward on the end of the plank. *Gradually increase the interval of time* that elapses before you place the food reward on the end of the plank. At the same time, you may *begin increasing your distance from the dog.* Always follow a parallel path to the dogwalk until you reach the end of the plank and always place the food on the plank. Carry the food in your outside hand; that is, the hand farthest away from the dog and the dogwalk. Do *not* use a verbal command like *Wait*—the dog is expected to stop at the end of the plank of his own volition. If the dog does so, he gets food. If the dog doesn't stop, pick up the dog and put him back on the plank.

3. The dog is not permitted to leave the plank until released.

NOTE: Reward the dog alternatively with the food on the plank and with the food from the hand.

Do not continue to Phase 9 unless the dog is focusing on the end of the plank and waiting for release before leaving the plank.

Phase 9: Release Before Reward

The dog should be off-lead. Have the food reward in hand.

1. Start the dog *from the ground.*

2. Command the dog to *Walk!* and allow him to ascend the plank. Signal to the end of the down plank to encourage the dog to focus downward. Do *not* use a verbal command like *Wait*—the dog is expected to stop at the end of the plank of his own volition.

3. Once the dog has paused at the end of the plank, release him with a quiet *Okay, Walk!* command. Give the dog the food reward *two steps beyond* the end of the plank.

NOTE: The purpose of this phase is to demonstrate to the dog that if commanded to do so, it is permissible to leave the plank without a food reward. Do not repeat this step multiple times as it contradicts the basic premise of this program, which is to reward the dog for being in the contact zone.

Do not continue to Phase 10 unless the dog is focusing on the end of the plank and waiting for release before leaving the plank.

Phase 10: The First Sequence

The dog should be off-lead. Have a food reward waiting at the end of the plank *and* in hand.

1. Set up a pipe tunnel in a "U"-shaped configuration about 10' from the end of the plank.

2. Start the dog *from the ground.*

3. Command the dog to *Walk!* and allow him to ascend the plank. Signal to the waiting food to encourage the dog to focus downward to the end of the plank. Do *not* use a verbal command like *Wait*—the dog is expected to stop at the end of the plank of his own volition. If the dog does so, he gets food. If the dog doesn't stop, pick up the dog and put him back on the plank.

4. Once the dog has paused and been rewarded, release him with a quiet *Okay, Tunnel!* command. Remember, the dog is not permitted to leave the plank until released.

5. Give the dog quiet praise and a food reward as the dog exits the tunnel.

Do not continue to Phase 11 unless the dog demonstrates his willingness to focus on the end of the plank, receive his reward, and then await release before being sent on to the tunnel.

Phase 11: No Pause

The dog should be off-lead. You should have the food reward in hand.

1. Start the dog *from the ground.*

2. Command the dog to *Walk!* and allow him to ascend the plank. Signal to the end of the plank to encourage the dog to focus downward.

3. As the dog reaches the end of the plank, *before pausing,* he is released with a quiet *Okay, Walk!* command. Give the dog the food reward *two steps beyond* the end of the plank.

Do not continue to the next phase unless the dog demonstrates that he is focusing on the end of the plank. The goal is that the timing of the release will result in a dog that pauses imperceptibly as he descends the down plank before being released.

Phase 12: Competition

After the dog is reliably pausing in the contact zone in competition, the *Okay!* command is omitted. The dog is released as he traverses the contact zone by giving him the next appropriate obstacle or directional command.

It is important that you continue to signal to the dog as if there may be a food reward waiting on the end of the plank, to encourage the dog to focus downward to the end of the plank.

You may encourage the dog to ascend the dogwalk and traverse the center plank as fast as possible, confident that the dog will pause imperceptibly on the down contact zone and flow onto the next obstacle when directed.

NOTE: During training, intermittently reinforce the dog with a food reward on the plank, from the hand, and two steps beyond the plank; and sometimes no food reward at all. In actual competition, the dog can be released as soon as a paw touches the contact zone when saving time is important. If time is not a factor, the dog occasionally should be expected to descend the plank all the way to the end and pause until released. The goal of this program is to *pattern the desired performance,* not to train the dog to expect food on the end of the plank.

Training the A-Frame

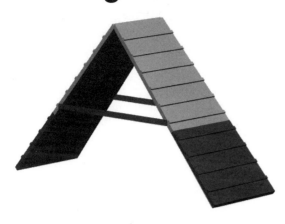

The desired performance of the A-frame can be described as follows:

- The dog ascends the obstacle in the direction indicated by the course flow.

- The dog must touch the yellow contact zone on the ascent.

- The dog must touch the yellow contact zone on the descent.

Performances that are faulted include:

Refusal

A dog is deemed to have refused the A-frame in several circumstances:

- If the dog crosses the run-out planes defined for the obstacle. The plane for the A-frame is the back edge of the contact zone on the ascent ramp. If the dog has to back up or turn around to ascend the ramp, it is a refusal.

- If the dog commits to the obstacle and gets back off before starting descent.

- If the dog advances towards the obstacle, focuses on the obstacles, and turns back. It's possible that a handler could cause this fault by calling the dog away from the A-frame after the dog has clearly committed towards it.

Missed Contact

A missed contact is incurred when the dog fails to touch either the ascent side or descent side safety contact zones. These are usually painted yellow. In some agility organizations (such as NADAC), it is not considered a fault to miss the ascent side contact zone. However, it is certainly a mistake not to train the dog to always hit the up-side contact.

Failure to Perform

Failure to perform is earned when the dog omits the A-frame.

Off-Course

An off-course is incurred when a dog performs the A-frame in the wrong direction, that is, in a direction other than the one determined by the judge.

Safety Rule

In the USDAA Starters level, and at all levels of AKC competition, if the dog commits to the A-frame with all four paws and then jumps off, the dog and handler are required to skip the obstacle and continue with the course. They will earn a failure to perform fault for this. If the dog is allowed to get back on the obstacle by his handler, the dog and handler will be immediately excused from the ring.

The A-Frame: A Control Obstacle

by Linda Mecklenburg

When training the A-frame, it is important for the dog to learn to perform the obstacle in a controlled manner. All dogs, especially the smaller ones, should be taught that it is possible to ascend the A-frame from a standstill and climb slat by slat.

Dogs must also be taught how to control their descent and not let their momentum drive them forward out of control. For these training sessions, it is essential to lower the A-frame to approximately 4-1/2'.

Up Ramp

The handler coaxes the dog up the ramp with a food motivator. Have a spotter on the opposite side to assist. The spotter should have *loose* hold on the buckle collar or tab. Encourage the dog to climb. If the dog accomplishes the task easily, the height of the A-frame may be raised. If not, it may be necessary to demonstrate to the dog that he must reach forward with a paw to gain purchase on a slat. If necessary, move each paw for the dog.

The most common problem is that as the dog nears the top he will lean backward on the spotter's hand in the collar. Do not allow the dog to do this. The purpose of the hand in the collar is only to prevent the dog from turning around, not for support. Make the dog do the work. Do *not* allow the dog to turn and descend the ramp if he gets frustrated; merely lift him off if he seems truly unable to climb. In this case, the A-frame must be lowered further.

Once the dog reaches the apex, reward.

All dogs should be confident in climbing the A-frame slat by slat because there are many instances where the dog may not have momentum to assist him.

Down Ramp

Consider yourself descending a steep incline (as a matter of fact, go out right now and try the A-frame at full height). You can either shift your weight back and take slow, controlled steps or you can lean forward and let momentum propel you forward.

Many dogs that have difficulty slowing on the down ramp of the A-frame fall into the second category—they are careening forward with uncontrolled momentum (see Figure 1). Handlers frequently admonish their dogs for missing the contact zone after they descend in this manner, when in actuality the dog could not have slowed no matter how hard he tried. Dogs must be *taught* to shift their weight back, collect themselves, and control their descent (see Figure 2).

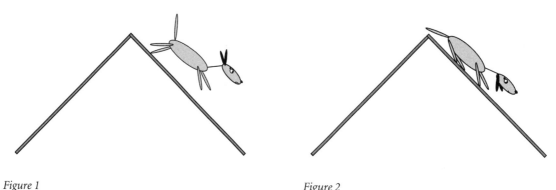

Figure 1   *Figure 2*

With the dog on a 6' lead, have the dog ascend the A-frame. Use whatever means the dog will respond to in order to get him to slow at the apex (*Easy!* or *Wait!* command, a lead check, and so on). The dog does not have to *stop* at the apex; however, it is helpful to minimize the forward momentum with which the dog begins his descent. From the apex, the dog is coaxed slowly forward and is rewarded at the bottom of the ramp with a food reward. If the dog leaves the ramp in an uncontrolled manner, immediately pick him up and lift him back onto the down ramp at the point where he jumped off.

Do not use a *Wait!* command at the bottom of the ramp. A common mistake is for the handler to command the dog to *Wait!* just as he reaches the contact zone, which is far too late for the dog to realistically stop. The result is a dog that stops with the front end, but somersaults forward with the rear (Figure 3).

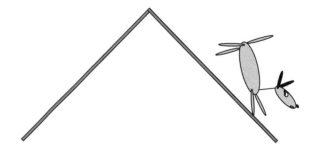

Figure 3

The dog is expected to learn to stop of his own volition. Do not allow him to leave the ramp without a release command. Holding this position may require some degree of effort on the dog's part. Reward. Release the dog with a quiet *Okay!* and allow him to walk off the obstacle.

Now that the dog has *incentive* to descend in a controlled manner (that is, positive reinforcement—the food— and negative reinforcement—being picked up and put back on the ramp), try again. Most dogs will naturally shift their weight back and descend in a collected, controlled manner if there is sufficient reason to do so; for others it's a learned technique.

A method that has proven useful is to lower the A-frame still further (some dogs require it to be flat on the ground) and lift the dog onto the middle of the down ramp. The dog is then commanded to *Down!* on the ramp. Once the dog is comfortable with this position, coax him forward one step, and then immediately *Down!* him again. Repeat until the dog reaches the bottom of the ramp. Reward, release, and walk the dog off the obstacle.

Artist: Jaci Cotton

This teaches the dog the body frame and *posture* required to accomplish a controlled descent. Watch a dog that is slowly descending the A-frame at full height; the dog will have its forelegs extended forward and hind legs tucked up in an almost prone position (Figure 2). It is not recommended to have the dog sit because this raises the center of gravity of the front end. Then in order for the dog to progress forward, he has to raise his rear end as well, which will result in the dog being propelled forward.

Once the dog is accustomed to a low body frame and the down posture that is required for a controlled descent, the height of the A-frame is gradually raised. Progress to having the dog ascend the A-frame, go up and over the apex and *Down!* just over the top, coax forward and *Down!*, coax forward and *Down!* until the bottom is reached.

Some dogs try to rise to a full standing position when asked to move forward. Use slight pressure on the dog's back to discourage this. It is important to have the dog's body remain as low to the ramp as possible. Reward and release. Continue raising the height of the obstacle.

Gradually phase out all of the downs, except one in the contact zone; although ultimately this one may be omitted as well. Remember to reward the dog for making the effort to control his descent and pausing at the bottom, and to correct him if he leaves the ramp without being released.

The dog must understand that there is a compelling reason to come down the steep ramp in a collected, controlled manner. Once you've demonstrated to him how to accomplish this, he can then reasonably be expected to perform the obstacle correctly.

Training the See-Saw

The desired performance of the see-saw can be described as follows:

- The dog ascends the obstacle in the direction indicated by the course flow.

- The dog must touch the yellow contact zone on the ascent.

- The dog must cross the pivot point to tip the plank to the ground.

- The dog must touch the yellow contact zone on the descent.

Performances that are faulted include:

Refusal	A dog is deemed to have refused the see-saw in several circumstances:

- If the dog crosses the run-out planes defined for the obstacle. The plane for the see-saw is the back edge of the contact zone on the ascent ramp. If the dog has to back up or turn around to ascend the plank, it is a refusal.

- If the dog commits to the obstacle and gets back off before starting descent.

- If the dog advances towards the obstacle, focuses on the obstacles, and turns back. It's possible that a handler could cause this fault by calling the dog away from the see-saw after the dog has clearly committed towards it.

Missed Contact	A missed contact is incurred when the dog fails to touch either the ascent side or descent side contact zones. These are usually painted yellow.
Failure to Perform	Failure to perform is earned when the dog omits the see-saw.
Fly-Off	A fly-off is incurred if the dog leaves the obstacle before the plank touches the ground or if the judge deems that the dog was not in control of the plank after crossing the pivot point.
Safety Rule	In the USDAA Starters level, and at all levels of AKC competition, if the dog commits to the see-saw with all four paws and then jumps off, the dog and handler are required to skip the obstacle and continue with the course. They will earn a failure to perform fault for this omission. If the dog is allowed to get back on the obstacle by his handler, the dog and handler will be immediately excused from the ring.

Walking the Plank: The Teeter

by Linda Mecklenburg

Success in teaching or retraining the teeter and getting a fast, accurate performance, rests in your patience and ability to be consistent in the application of positive and negative reinforcement. This training program relies on two fundamental rules:

1. The dog is rewarded with food treats and praise for being in the contact zone.

2. The dog is corrected for leaving the contact zone (simply by picking up the dog and putting him back on the end of the plank) without a command from the handler.

The desired outcome of this program is a dog that races up and over the teeter in complete control of the plank. The dog pauses imperceptibly in the contact zone and then proceeds ahead on course as directed.

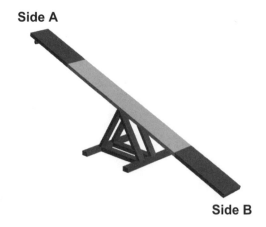

Side A

Side B

Introductory Agility Workbook

Important Training Note

For the purposes of explaining this training method, it is necessary to differentiate the two ends of the teeter plank. Since it's difficult to define an "up-side" and "down-side" on the teeter because of the nature of the obstacle, this program refers to the end of the plank that normally rests on the ground as Side B; and refers to the end of the plank that is in the air as Side A. Please refer to the diagram on the preceding page for clarification.

In the initial phases of training, you will essentially be using the teeter backwards from the way it would normally be performed—that is, you will be lifting the dog onto the plank and placing him on the end of the plank that is already resting on the ground. It is much easier to perform the obstacle this way, rather than having a spotter tip and hold the plank to the ground so you can put the dog on the other end. You also don't have to worry about the possibility of the plank coming up if the dog steps off the side. The only time the dog must perform the teeter in the "proper" direction, is when you start working the complete obstacle from the ground. During the other phases of training, the teeter will look the same to the dog whether he's going up the "down ramp" or down the "up ramp".

Phase 1: First Contact

The dog should be wearing a buckle collar and a short tab. The collar and tab allow you to control the dog on the plank. Have a food reward ready in hand. A spotter on the side opposite the handler may be useful to steady the dog and increase its sense of security. The teeter does *not* move in this phase of training.

1. Lift the dog onto *the Side B end of the plank*, facing downward off the teeter, and reward him for remaining there with food and praise. The dog can be in any position but standing is preferred. At first the food is given directly to the dog; then it is placed on the end of the plank. Signal to the food by pointing to it with the hand closest to the dog and touching it, encouraging the dog to focus downward to the end of the plank.

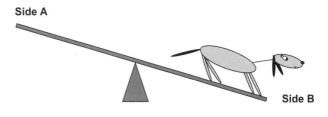

2. If the dog attempts to leave the plank, pick the dog up and put him back on the plank. Then reward the dog again for being in the contact zone.

3. The dog is not permitted to leave the plank until released with a quiet *Okay*. Do not praise the dog or celebrate as the dog leaves the plank. Do not use food or toys as the dog leaves the plank. Do not send the dog to another obstacle. *The dog should not associate leaving the plank with positive reinforcement—positive reinforcement should occur only in the contact zone.* The exercise ends when the dog leaves the plank. You may restart the exercise.

Do not continue to Phase 2 unless the dog is focusing on the end of the plank, anticipating the food reward, and waiting for release before leaving the plank.

Phase 2: Midway on the Plank

The dog should be wearing a buckle collar and a short tab. Have a food reward waiting on the end of the plank. A spotter on the side opposite the handler may be useful to steady the dog. The teeter does *not* move in this phase.

1. Lift the dog onto *the center of the plank*, facing downward off the teeter, towards the Side B end of the plank.

2. Command the dog to *Walk!* and then guide him forward. Signal to the waiting food to encourage the dog to focus downward to the end of the plank. Do *not* use a verbal command like *Wait*—the dog is expected to stop at the end of the plank of his own volition. If the dog does so, he gets food. If the dog doesn't stop, pick the dog up and put him back on the plank.

   NOTE: If you prefer to have your students use different commands for the dogwalk and the see-saw, you can use a word other than *Walk!* in these steps.

3. The dog is not permitted to leave the plank until released with a quiet *Okay*. The dog should not associate leaving the plank with positive reinforcement—positive reinforcement should occur only in the contact zone. The exercise ends when the dog leaves the plank.

Do not continue to Phase 3 unless the dog is focusing on the end of the plank, anticipating the food reward, and waiting for release before leaving the plank.

Phase 3: First Motion

The dog should be wearing a buckle collar and a short tab. Have a food reward waiting at the end of the plank. A spotter on the side opposite the handler may be useful to steady the dog. A second spotter will control the movement of the plank from *behind* the dog.

1. The spotter pushes down on the Side A end of the plank until the Side B end of the plank is 6" off the ground. Then, lift the dog onto *the center of the plank*, facing towards the Side B end of the plank.

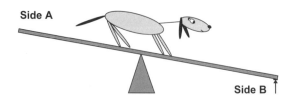

2. The spotter gently lowers the plank to the ground. The dog is praised and allowed to relax before proceeding.

3. Command the dog to *Walk!* and allow him to walk forward. Signal to the waiting food to encourage the dog to focus downward to the end of the plank. Do *not* use a verbal command like *Wait*—the dog is expected to stop at the end of the plank of his own volition. If the dog does so, he gets food. If the dog doesn't stop, pick the dog up and put him back on the plank.

4. The dog is not permitted to leave the plank until released with a quiet *Okay*. The dog should not associate leaving the plank with positive reinforcement—positive reinforcement should occur only in the contact zone. The exercise ends when the dog leaves the plank.

Do not continue to Phase 4 unless the dog is calmly accepting the motion of the plank, focusing on the end of the plank, anticipating the food reward, and waiting for release before leaving the plank.

Phase 4: Increased Motion

The dog should be wearing a buckle collar and a short tab. Have a food reward waiting at the end of the plank. A spotter on the side opposite the handler may be useful to steady the dog. A second spotter will control the movement of the plank from *behind* the dog.

1. The spotter pushes down on the Side A end of the plank until the Side B end of the plank is 12" off the ground. Then, lift the dog onto *the center of the plank*, facing towards the Side B end of the plank.

2. The spotter gently lowers the plank to the ground. The dog is praised and allowed to relax before proceeding.

3. Command the dog to *Walk!* and allow him to walk forward. Signal to the waiting food to encourage the dog to focus downward to the end of the plank. Do *not* use a verbal command like *Wait*—the dog is expected to stop at the end of the plank of his own volition. If the dog does so, he gets food. If the dog doesn't stop, pick the dog up and put him back on the plank.

4. The dog is not permitted to leave the plank until released with a quiet *Okay*. The dog should not associate leaving the plank with positive reinforcement—positive reinforcement should occur only in the contact zone. The exercise ends when the dog leaves the plank.

Do not continue to Phase 5 unless the dog is calmly accepting the motion of the plank, focusing on the end of the plank, anticipating the food reward, and waiting for release before leaving the plank.

Phase 5: More Motion on the Plank

The dog should be wearing a buckle collar and a short tab. Have a food reward waiting at the end of the plank. A spotter on the side opposite the handler may be useful to steady the dog. A second spotter will control the movement of the plank from *behind* the dog.

1. The spotter pushes down on the Side A end of the plank until the plank is parallel to the ground. Then, lift the dog onto *the center of the plank*, facing towards the Side B end of the plank.

   NOTE: Since most teeters are 24" high at the pivot point, you can help out the spotter by placing a 24" table under the end of the plank that he is working. By pushing down on the plank until it meets the table, the spotter can easily hold the plank steady as the dog is being lifted onto the plank.

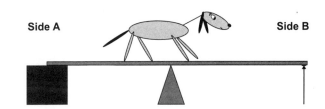

2. The spotter gently lowers the plank to the ground. The dog is praised and allowed to relax before proceeding.

3. Command the dog to *Walk!* and allow him to walk forward. Signal to the waiting food to encourage the dog to focus on the end of the plank. Do *not* use a verbal command like *Wait*—the dog is expected to stop at the end of the plank of his own volition. If the dog does so, he gets food. If the dog doesn't stop, pick the dog up and put him back on the plank.

4. The dog is not permitted to leave the plank until released with a quiet *Okay*. The dog should not associate leaving the plank with positive reinforcement—positive reinforcement should occur only in the contact zone. The exercise ends when the dog leaves the plank.

Do not continue to Phase 6 unless the dog is calmly accepting the motion of the plank, focusing on the end of the plank, anticipating the food reward, and waiting for release before leaving the plank.

Phase 6: Walk Into the Motion

The dog should be wearing a buckle collar and a short tab. Have a food reward waiting at the end of the plank. A spotter on the side opposite the handler may be useful to steady the dog and increase its sense of security. A second spotter will control the movement of the plank from *behind* the dog.

1. The spotter pushes down on the Side A end of the plank until the plank is parallel to the ground. (You can use a table to help the spotter support the plank.) Then, lift the dog onto *the Side A end of the plank*, facing towards the Side B end of the plank.

2. Command the dog to *Walk!* and allow him to walk forward. Signal to the waiting food to encourage the dog to focus on the end of the plank. The spotter gently lowers the plank to the ground as the dog passes the pivot point. The dog is praised and allowed to relax before proceeding. The dog is *not* encouraged to come to a complete stop at the pivot point unless the motion of the teeter frightens him.

3. The dog is encouraged to continue walking forward slowly. Signal to the waiting food to encourage the dog to focus downward to the end of the plank. Do *not* use a verbal command like *Wait*—the dog is expected to stop at the end of the plank of his own volition. If the dog does so, he gets food. If the dog doesn't stop, pick the dog up and put him back on the plank.

4. The dog is not permitted to leave the plank until released with a quiet *Okay*. The dog should not associate leaving the plank with positive reinforcement—positive reinforcement should occur only in the contact zone. The exercise ends when the dog leaves the plank.

Do not continue to Phase 7 unless the dog is calmly accepting the motion of the plank, focusing on the end of the plank, anticipating the food reward, and waiting for release before leaving the plank.

Phase 7: The Dog Controls the Motion

The dog should be wearing a buckle collar and a short tab. Have a food reward waiting at the end of the plank. A spotter on the side opposite the handler may be useful to steady the dog and increase its sense of security. A second spotter will control the movement of the plank from *behind* the dog.

1. The spotter pushes down on the Side A end of the plank until the plank is parallel to the ground. (You can use a table to help the spotter support the plank.) Then, lift the dog onto *the Side A end of the plank,* facing towards the Side B end of the plank.

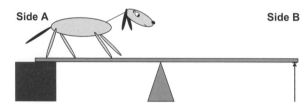

2. Command the dog to *Walk!* and allow him to walk forward. Signal to the waiting food to encourage the dog to focus on the end of the plank. The spotter should allow *the dog* to lower the plank to the ground as the dog passes the pivot point. The dog is praised and allowed to relax before proceeding. The dog is *not* encouraged to come to a complete stop at the pivot point unless the motion of the teeter frightens him.

3. The dog is encouraged to continue walking forward slowly. Signal to the waiting food to encourage the dog to focus downward to the end of the plank. Do *not* use a verbal command like *Wait*—the dog is expected to stop at the end of the plank of his own volition. If the dog does so, he gets food. If the dog doesn't stop, pick the dog up and put him back on the plank.

4. The dog is not permitted to leave the plank until released with a quiet *Okay*. The dog should not associate leaving the plank with positive reinforcement—positive reinforcement should occur only in the contact zone. The exercise ends when the dog leaves the plank.

Do not continue to Phase 8 unless the dog is calmly initiating and accepting the motion of the plank, focusing on the end of the plank, anticipating the food reward, and waiting for release before leaving the plank.

Phase 8: From the Ground

The dog should be on-lead. Have a food reward waiting at the end of the plank. A spotter on the side opposite the handler may be useful to steady the dog and increase its sense of security. A second spotter should be ready to come in *behind* the dog and gently lower the plank to the ground as the dog passes the pivot point, *if necessary*.

1. Start the dog *from the ground at the Side B end of the plank.*

2. Command the dog to *Walk!* and allow him to walk forward. Signal to the waiting food to encourage the dog to focus on the end of the plank. The spotter should allow *the dog* to lower the plank to the ground as he passes the pivot point. The dog is praised and allowed to relax before proceeding. The dog is *not* encouraged to come to a complete stop at the pivot point unless the motion of the teeter frightens him.

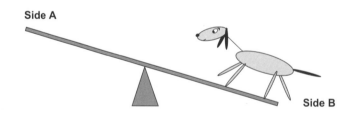

3. The dog is encouraged to continue walking forward slowly. Signal to the waiting food to encourage the dog to focus downward to the end of the plank. Do *not* use a verbal command like *Wait*—the dog is expected to stop at the end of the plank of his own volition. If the dog does so, he gets food. If the dog doesn't stop, pick the dog up and put him back on the plank.

4. The dog is not permitted to leave the plank until released with a quiet *Okay*. The dog should not associate leaving the plank with positive reinforcement—positive reinforcement should occur only in the contact zone. The exercise ends when the dog leaves the plank.

Do not continue to Phase 9 unless the dog is calmly initiating and accepting the motion of the plank, focusing on the end of the plank, anticipating the food reward, and waiting for release before leaving the plank.

Phase 9: Off-Lead

The dog should be off-lead. Have a food reward waiting at the end of the plank. A spotter should be ready to come in *behind* the dog and gently lower the plank to the ground, *if necessary*. Gradually phase out the spotter opposite the handler.

1. Start the dog *from the ground at the Side B end of the plank.*

2. Command the dog to *Walk!* and allow him to walk forward. Signal to the waiting food to encourage the dog to focus on the end of the plank. The spotter should allow *the dog* to lower the plank to the ground as the dog passes the pivot point. The dog is praised and allowed to relax before proceeding. The dog is *not* encouraged to come to a complete stop at the pivot point unless the motion of the teeter frightens him.

3. The dog is encouraged to continue walking forward slowly. Signal to the waiting food to encourage the dog to focus downward to the end of the plank. Do *not* use a verbal command like *Wait*—the dog is expected to stop at the end of the plank of his own volition. If the dog does so, he gets food. If the dog doesn't stop, pick the dog up and put him back on the plank.

4. The dog is not permitted to leave the plank until released with a quiet *Okay*. The dog should not associate leaving the plank with positive reinforcement—positive reinforcement should occur only in the contact zone. The exercise ends when the dog leaves the plank.

Do not continue to Phase 10 unless the dog is calmly initiating and accepting the motion of the plank, focusing on the end of the plank, anticipating the food reward, and waiting for release before leaving the plank.

Phase 10: Food in Hand

The dog should be off-lead. Have a food reward ready in hand, rather than leaving it at the end of the plank. A spotter should be ready to come in *behind* the dog and gently lower the plank, *if necessary*.

1. Start the dog *from the ground at the Side B end of the plank.*

2. Command the dog to *Walk!* and allow him to walk forward. Signal to the end of the plank with your inside hand (the hand closest to the dog), actually touching the end of the plank. The spotter should allow *the dog* to lower the plank to the ground as the dog passes the pivot point.

3. The dog is encouraged to continue walking forward slowly. Signal to the end of the plank to encourage the dog to focus. As the dog approaches the zone, *wait for the dog to pause,* and then *immediately* place the food on the end of the plank. Carry the food in your outside hand; that is, the hand farthest away from the dog and the teeter. Do *not* use a verbal command like *Wait*—the dog is expected to stop at the *end* of the plank of his own volition. If the dog does so, he gets food. If the dog doesn't stop, pick the dog up and put him back on the plank.

4. The dog is not permitted to leave the plank until released with a quiet *Okay*. The dog should not associate leaving the plank with positive reinforcement—positive reinforcement should occur only in the contact zone. The exercise ends when the dog leaves the plank.

Do not continue to Phase 11 unless the dog is calmly initiating and accepting the motion of the plank, focusing on the end of the plank, anticipating the food reward, and waiting for release before leaving the plank.

Phase 11: Increased Time and Distance

The dog should be off-lead. Have a food reward ready in hand, rather than leaving it at the end of the plank. A spotter should be ready to come in *behind* the dog and gently lower the plank, *if necessary*. The dog is *not* ready for this phase of training if it is fearful of the plank's motion.

1. Start the dog *from the ground at the Side B end of the plank.*

2. Command the dog to *Walk!* and allow him to walk forward. Signal to the end of the plank with your inside hand (the hand closest to the dog), actually touching the end of the plank. The spotter should allow *the dog* to lower the plank to the ground as the dog passes the pivot point.

3. The dog is encouraged to continue walking forward slowly. Signal to the end of the plank to encourage the dog to focus downward. As the dog approaches the zone, wait for the dog to pause, and then place the food reward on the end of the plank. *Gradually increase the interval of time* that elapses before you place the food reward on the end of the plank. At the same time, you may *begin increasing your distance from the dog.* Always follow a parallel path to the teeter until you reach the end of the plank and always place the food on the plank. Carry the food in your outside hand; that is, the hand farthest away from the dog and the teeter. Do *not* use a verbal command like *Wait*—the dog is expected to stop at the end of the plank of his own volition. If the dog does so, he gets food. If the dog doesn't stop, pick the dog up and put him back on the plank.

4. The dog is not permitted to leave the plank until released with a quiet *Okay*. The dog should not associate leaving the plank with positive reinforcement—positive reinforcement should occur only in the contact zone. The exercise ends when the dog leaves the plank.

NOTE: Reward the dog alternatively with the food on the plank and with the food from the hand.

Do not continue to Phase 12 unless the dog is calmly initiating and accepting the motion of the plank, focusing on the end of the plank, anticipating the food reward, and waiting for release before leaving the plank.

Phase 12: Release Before Reward

The dog should be off-lead for this phase. Have a food reward ready in hand, rather than leaving it at the end of the plank. A spotter should be ready to come in *behind* the dog and gently lower the plank, *if necessary*. However, you will gradually phase out this spotter. The dog is *not* ready for this phase of training if he's fearful of the plank's motion.

1. Start the dog *from the ground at the Side B end of the plank.*

2. Command the dog to *Walk!* and allow him to walk forward. Signal to the end of the plank with your inside hand (the hand closest to the dog), actually touching the end of the plank.

3. The dog is encouraged to continue walking forward slowly. Signal to the end of the plank to encourage the dog to focus downward. As the dog approaches the zone, wait for the dog to pause. Do *not* use a verbal command like *Wait*—the dog is expected to stop at the end of the plank of his own volition. If the dog does so, he gets food. If the dog doesn't stop, pick the dog up and put him back on the plank.

4. Once the dog has paused, release him a quiet *Okay, Walk!* command. Carry the food in your outside hand; that is, the hand farthest away from the dog and the teeter. Give the dog the food reward two steps beyond the end of the plank. Remember, the dog is not permitted to leave the plank until released.

NOTE: The purpose of this phase is to demonstrate to the dog that if commanded to do so, it is permissible to leave the plank without a food reward. Do not repeat this step multiple times as it contradicts the basic premise of this program, which is to reward the dog for being in the contact zone.

Do not continue to Phase 13 unless the dog is calmly initiating and accepting the motion of the plank, focusing on the end of the plank, anticipating the food reward, and waiting for release before leaving the plank.

Phase 13: The First Sequence

The dog should be off-lead. Have a food reward waiting at the end of the plank *and* in hand.

1. Set up a pipe tunnel in a "U"-shaped configuration about 10' from the end of the plank.

2. Start the dog *from the ground at the Side B end of the plank.*

3. Command the dog to *Walk!* and allow him to ascend the plank. Signal to the waiting food to encourage the dog to focus downward to the end of the plank. Do *not* use a verbal command like *Wait*—the dog is expected to stop at the end of the plank of his own volition. If the dog does so, he gets food. If the dog doesn't stop, pick the dog up and put him back on the plank.

4. Once the dog has paused and been rewarded, release him with a quiet *Okay, Tunnel!* command. Remember, the dog is not permitted to leave the plank until released.

5. Give the dog quiet praise and a food reward as the dog exits the tunnel.

Do not continue to Phase 14 unless the dog demonstrates his willingness to focus on the end of the plank, receive his reward, and then wait for release before being sent on to the tunnel.

Phase 14: No Pause

The dog should be off-lead. Have the food reward ready in hand.

1. Start the dog *from the ground at the Side B end of the plank.*

2. Command the dog to *Walk!* and allow him to walk forward. Signal to the end of the plank to encourage the dog to focus downward.

3. As the dog reaches the end of the plank, *before pausing*, he is released with a quiet *Okay, Walk!* command. Give the dog the food reward two steps beyond the end of the plank.

Do not continue to the next phase unless the dog demonstrates that he is continuing to focus on the end of the plank. The goal is that the timing of the release will result in a dog that pauses imperceptibly as he descends the plank before being released.

Phase 15: Competition

After the dog is reliably pausing in the contact zone in competition, the *Okay!* command is omitted. The dog is released as he traverses the contact zone by giving him the next appropriate obstacle or directional command.

It is important that you continue to signal to the dog as if there may be a food reward waiting on the end of the plank, to encourage the dog to focus downward to the end of the plank.

You may encourage the dog to ascend the teeter and traverse the plank as fast as possible, as long as control of the plank is maintained. The dog should pause imperceptibly on the down contact zone and flow onto the next obstacle when directed.

NOTE: During training, intermittently reinforce the dog with a food reward on the plank, from the hand, and two steps beyond the plank; and sometimes no food reward at all. In actual competition, the dog can be released as soon as a paw touches the contact zone when saving time is important. If time is not a factor, the dog occasionally should be expected to descend the plank all the way to the end and pause until released. The goal of this program is to *pattern the desired performance*, not to train the dog to expect food on the end of the plank.

Training the Weave Poles

The desired performance of the weave poles can be described as follows:

- The dog enters the poles from right to left between the first and second poles.

- The dog turns right after each even numbered pole, and turns left after each odd numbered poles.

- The dog should work briskly down the series of poles, weaving in and out until all poles have been performed.

Performances that are faulted include:

Refusal

A dog is deemed to have refused the weave poles if it crosses one of two run-out planes defined for the obstacle. As shown in Figure 1, the plane is perpendicular to pole 1 if the dog passes to the left of that pole; the plane is perpendicular to pole 2 if the dog passes to the right of that pole.

Many judges will fault the refusal if the dog has to back up to make a correct entry.

Missed Pole

A missed pole is incurred when the dog goes beyond the point where he should have turned to weave around a pole in the sequence. In Figure 2, the dog has missed pole 3.

Many judges will fault the missed pole if the dog has to back up to make the correction.

Under AKC rules a missed pole is faulted as a refusal.

Improper Entry

An improper entry is when the dog enters between the wrong poles—either the dog has made a left to right entry (as shown in Figure 3), or makes the entry after pole 2.

Under AKC rules an improper entry is faulted as a refusal.

Off-Course

An off-course is incurred when a dog performs the weave poles in the wrong direction; that is, in a direction other than the one determined by the judge.

This can happen especially in performance of the weave poles when a dog has faulted the poles in some other way and the handler calls the dog back to start again. If the dog sets up *any* weaving motion going back to the handler as shown in Figure 4, the dog has incurred an off-course.

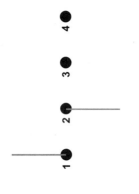

Figure 1   Figure 2   Figure 3   Figure 4

APPENDIX

Methods of Training the Poles

There are four distinct methods of teaching the weave poles. Your training program will likely adopt one of these methods. Each method is described in the sections that follow.

Leaning Poles Method

This is the method referred to throughout this workbook. We subscribe to the leaning poles as the most effective means of teaching a dog to weave.

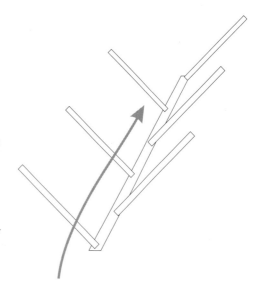

The leaning poles method usually requires a "prop" obstacle. The poles need to be hinged along the base so that they can be pivoted alternately left and then right at a severe angle. However, it is possible to use some kind of pound-in-the-ground weave poles that can be set up (pounded in) on angles prior to class.

Patience is the key when using this training method. It is unlikely that any but the most extraordinary dogs will learn to weave reliably in an eight-week class—though success is more likely if the dog's handler owns a set of leaning poles at home.

When the dog is introduced to the obstacle, the poles are laid out at 90°—that's lying flat on the ground. The dog is trotted down the middle of the poles once or twice, and then thee poles are raised so that the tips are about 12" off the ground. The dogs are trotted back and forth through them again.

In the second week, the poles begin at 12" off the ground but are quickly raised so they're leaning 45° off center. And then in subsequent weeks, the poles are raised only a couple of inches at a time. At the end of an eight-week course, the poles should *still* be leaning at about 30° off center.

NOTE: In most cases, you will find that the angle of the poles will need to be greater for little dogs than for big dogs. If you consider that a little dog's line of vision might be a foot below a big dog's line of vision, the big dog may see a wide gap in the poles ahead of him while the little dog sees only a narrow gap. So while the big dogs may be comfortable working with the poles at a 30° angle by the end of the program, the little dogs may be working at 40°.

Channel Wire Method

The channel wire method requires a "prop". The wires are connected to small pipes that can be slipped over the poles. The odd poles are connected and the even poles are connected so that the dog has a perfect channel, defined by the wires, down the length of the weave pole set.

In an introductory agility class, it is unlikely that the wires should ever come off of the weave poles. That is really a project for a more intermediate class. However, if you really want to test the dog's understanding of the poles, you might try taking off the wires that connect the even poles in the seventh or eighth week of class. This would allow the handler to be in the control position to push the dog back in between the poles after each odd numbered obstacle. The wire will control the dog from running out on the side away from the handler.

Some dogs will try to jump over the wires or run under them. To prevent this, you could use two sets of wires so that they guard against the dog passing through high and low. In any case, if a dog is trying to jump or crawl out of the channel, it is a clear indication that the handler should still be controlling the dog through the poles by using a short tab.

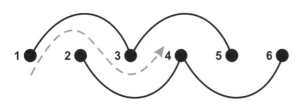

NOTE: The channel wires method can be combined with the chute method, described below. That's kind of like the man who wears both a belt *and* suspenders, a bit on the insecure side. But worth a shot for dogs that are having problems with the poles.

Chute Method

The chute method is very much like the leaning poles method, except the poles are straight up. The odd poles are staggered away from the even poles so that to the dog's eyes the poles form an alternating chute of poles on the dog's left and right.

Gradually, the poles should be pushed closer together. It is only when the chute is narrower than the dog's shoulders that you should perceive any kind of weaving motion.

For that reason, it's worth noting that this training method is different for big dogs than for little dogs. If all dogs are performing the same chute, you'll find the big dogs being required to actually begin weaving before the little dogs are so required.

Again, you shouldn't be in a big hurry with this method. In the course of an eight-week class, the poles will never be pushed together in a straight line. There should always be a chute big enough for all dogs to see through.

Push Me/Pull Me

This method is nothing more than leading the dog through the weave poles to show him the desired path. At first, the dog is led through the poles on-lead. Later on in training, the dog is led through with a food treat or a toy. The handler should use his own footwork and body motion to aid the dog in figuring out which way to move through the poles.

A low set of poles, no more than 24" high, is useful. This allows the handler to easily reach and control the dog between the poles.

If you are going to use this method of teaching the poles, the handler will be required *always* to be at his dog's side. It is obvious that you won't be able to do some of the exercises in this book, like calling your dog through the poles. You will be able to work both sides of the dog simply by controlling the dog with a lead.

In any event, have patience. Not too many dogs will learn to weave given one hour a week, over eight weeks. A more intensive weave pole program will be required at the intermediate level.

The Lofthouse Law of "Weavies" for Large Breeds
by Kathryn Lofthouse

Artist: Jaci Cotton

When training larger dogs in agility, it should be borne in mind that a larger dog can only weave at the fastest pace possible for him, according to his size and body length. The physical stress and difficulty of weave pole performance at optimum speed will magnify in relation to the size of the dog.

One should strive for optimum weave pole performance for the size, length, and breed of dog. It would be sad to see somebody constantly striving for a faster weave pole performance from a dog who was doing all he was physically able to do, that is, weaving as fast as a dog of his size could go. Obviously, the weaves are a lot easier for the dog who simply must learn to hop from side to side without bending his whole body, but then the common answer to that, as I'm sure you know, is to get a smaller dog... for those who don't want a smaller dog just let your dog do the best he can and be happy!

A Philosophy for Training to Win

by Monica Percival

In preparation for a seminar several years ago, someone asked me to put together a list of what I thought went into "training a dog to win" in agility. I think the person expected a laundry list of agility skills to work on; instead, she got the list below. While many of these principles may seem to state the obvious or be messages that we strive to communicate to our students in every class, I find that it's helpful for students to have a handout like this that they can take home and think about from time to time.

- **Maintain a positive attitude.** You help shape your dog's attitude with the attitude that you project. A happy dog is an enthusiastic worker who is willing to accept challenges!

- **Have fun.** If you aren't having fun, your dog isn't having fun. Success on the agility field is not a life and death issue. Have you ever met a dog that cared whether or not he got a qualifying score?

- **Dogs are "only human."** Dogs make mistakes and have bad days just like us. When your dog makes a mistake, don't jump too quickly to blame him. Look at what you might have done to cause the error (such as giving a late command or standing in the wrong position). Think about what you could have done to prevent the dog from making the mistake. Evaluate whether or not the dog really understands what you expect of him.

- **Agility is a team sport.** You and your dog must work together. You are the team captain.

- **No harsh corrections.** Harsh corrections can destroy a dog's confidence. No praise should be the harshest correction you ever give.

- **A dog in top physical condition has an easier road to achieving top performance.** A top tennis player must have more than a killer serve and a great forehand to win—he must have strength, endurance, flexibility, timing, balance, and coordination. While we're born with some measure of these abilities, we can enhance them with regular exercise. The same holds true for dogs...Agility requires greater overall physical fitness than what can be achieved by just working the obstacles. As with people, a regular exercise program will help increase your dog's strength and endurance, improve his concentration, keep him from becoming overweight, prevent injuries ("soft" muscles are more prone to injury), and make him feel better overall.

- **Every dog needs different training.** If this isn't the first dog you are training for agility, recognize that every dog is different and what worked for your other dog may not work for this dog.

- **Set achievable goals in both training and competition.** Setting realistic goals allows both you and your dog to achieve success in every training session and every competitive class you enter—success builds confidence! If your goals aren't realistic, you will constantly be frustrated with your dog and the dog may lose interest in agility. Don't let the success of other people's dogs cause you to set goals that your dog can't achieve—just because Fido learned the weave poles in a month doesn't mean that Rover can.

- **There are no shortcuts.** Just as a child can't progress from learning the alphabet to reading *War and Peace* overnight, a dog cannot progress from performing individual obstacles to running courses overnight. Slowly increase the number of obstacles you ask him to perform in sequence. Likewise, you cannot start teaching your dog to work at a distance by trying to send him 20' to the tunnel. It's important to build good basic agility skills that you can fall back on when you have a training problem in the future. If you try to take shortcuts in training, it will catch up with you later when you try to do more advanced work with your dog.

- **The training process never ends!** Just because your dog did a particular exercise right yesterday, doesn't mean he'll remember how to do it right today or tomorrow. Even when a dog is competing successfully, you'll always run into new problems—such as the dog that forgets what a contact zone is or thinks it's better to begin weaving at the second pole. That's the challenge of agility.

- **Don't be afraid to go back to basics.** If, for example, your dog is missing contact zones or has started refusing to perform an obstacle that he's done correctly for years, don't go searching for gimmicks or magical cures. Usually, solving the problem requires taking one or more steps backwards. Figuratively, you need to step back from the situation and try to analyze the problem objectively. Literally, you need to go back a step or more in your training program and make sure that the dog understands the "job". Sometimes, you'll even find that you need to start part of the training process all over again at step one. Many of us fight going backwards because we feel that there is some stigma attached to it or that we have failed in some way. Don't take it personally and don't fight it! Going back to basics can often be the quickest and easiest solution to a problem.

- **Introduce one challenge at a time.** You'll achieve greater success if you focus on teaching your dog one skill at a time. For example, if your dog is learning to weave with slanted poles and you want to teach him to enter the poles ahead of you, don't try increasing the angle of the poles and increasing distance between you and the dog at the same time. Instead, start by decreasing the angle of the poles to where the dog has been successful in the past. Run with the dog as he does the poles. Then on each subsequent performance, start hanging back a little bit at a time as the dog enters the poles. When you have built up to the distance you wanted to achieve (and this may take multiple training sessions), increase the angle of the poles and start by running with the dog again and then hanging back a little at a time.

- **Find out what motivates your dog.** A few dogs work just for the sake of working—however, this is the exception rather than the rule! Most dogs carefully weigh the cost versus the benefit of performing a particular task. These dogs need something to motivate them, especially while they are learning the basics of agility. You'll need to experiment to find out what turns on your dog—praise, cookies (and probably liver brownies or Rollover rather than Milk Bones!), a toy, or whatever works. With some dogs, you'll need to use a combination of tools to motivate the dog and you'll need to change the reward from time to time.

- **Know when to stop a training session.** It's important to stop each training session before your dog loses enthusiasm—very often this is before you, the handler, are ready to stop the training session. Learn to read your dog and know when his attention is waning. Before your dog has turned off, set up an exercise to end the session on a positive, successful note. If you are at a group practice, put your dog away in a quiet place and sit back and enjoy watching the other dogs train. You can learn a lot by watching other handlers and dogs work.

- **Know when you shouldn't start a training session.** If you are having a bad day and aren't able to be patient and project a positive attitude, don't start a training session—it doesn't matter if you only have access to equipment on that particular day. It's better to skip a training session than to experience failure because you can't hold up your end of the team or to inadvertently cause a future training problem because the dog associated your bad mood with a particular obstacle or exercise.

- **You don't need obstacles to train.** Many basic agility skills (such as wait, fast down, easy, and directional commands) can be taught at home without using any agility obstacles. Skill building and control exercises should be part of your daily routine.

- **Keep agility stress free.** Designing a training program that emphasizes the principles listed above will help create a stress-free learning environment for your dog. Remember, a dog that is stressed will shut down. This can be seen in the dog that runs laps around the course, leaves the course, sniffs around ignoring the handler, or refuses to perform the obstacles. Learn the strengths and weaknesses of your dog and learn how to get the most out of the dog without pushing him past his limits and stressing him out.

Dog Profile Form

1. Handler's Name: _____

2. Dog's Call Name: _____

3. Breed(s): _____

4. Age: _____ Height: _____ Weight: _____ Sex: _____

5. Has the dog been spayed or neutered? _____

6. Are you the primary owner of the dog? If not, what is your relationship to this dog? _____
   _____

7. How long have you owned the dog? _____

8. Where did you obtain the dog?

   ☐ Ad in Paper   ☐ Breeder   ☐ Friend or Relative

   ☐ Pet Store   ☐ Stray   ☐ Shelter

   ☐ Rescue Agency   ☐ Other: _____

9. When was the dog last seen by a vet? _____

10. Is the dog on any medication? What and why? _____
    _____

11. Does the dog get groomed? How often? _____

12. Where is the dog kept?

    ☐ In house loose   ☐ In house crated   ☐ In fenced yard

    ☐ In dog kennel   ☐ Tied outside   ☐ Other: _____

13. Has the dog ever bitten anyone? If so, please describe when this happened and the circumstances: _____
    _____
    _____

14. Has the dog ever been in a fight with another dog? If so, please describe how many times this has happened and the circumstances: _____
    _____
    _____

15. How does the dog react to:

    Men? _____

    Women? _____

    Children? _____

    Strangers? _____

    Crowds? _____

    Other adult dogs? _____

    Puppies? _____

16. What things upset this dog? _____

_____

17. How does the dog react to riding in a car? _____

18. How does the dog react to being left alone? _____

19. How would you describe the dog's personality? Check all that apply:

☐ Shy ☐ Friendly ☐ Fearful ☐ Happy

☐ Aggressive ☐ Playful ☐ Nervous ☐ Bored

☐ Hyperactive ☐ Loud ☐ Annoying ☐ Calm

☐ Jealous ☐ Submissive ☐ Territorial ☐ Finicky

☐ Indifferent ☐ Dominant ☐ Extroverted ☐ Dependent

20. What bad habits does your dog have? Check all that apply:

☐ Barks/howls ☐ Digs ☐ Chews ☐ Growls

☐ Runs away ☐ Jumps up ☐ Gets in trash ☐ Chases things

☐ Bites ☐ Wets ☐ Begs

☐ Other: _____

21. What commands does your dog respond to? Check all that apply:

☐ Come ☐ Don't Jump ☐ Down ☐ Drop It

☐ Enough ☐ Fetch ☐ Give ☐ Heel

☐ Hup ☐ In ☐ Leave It ☐ Let's Go

☐ Move ☐ Okay ☐ Sit ☐ Stand

☐ Stay ☐ Stop It ☐ Take It ☐ Wait

☐ Others: _____

22. How often will the dog come when called?

☐ 100% ☐ 75% ☐ 50% ☐ 25% ☐ 0%

23. Has the dog had prior agility training? _____

_____

24. List activities enjoyed by you and your dog: _____

_____

_____

25. List titles earned by your dog: _____

_____

_____

_____

26. List future goals you have for yourself and your dog: _____

_____

_____

_____

Agility Resource Sheet

To help you pursue your new hobby, here's a list of the various organizations that sponsor dog agility events, recommended agility reading and viewing selections, and companies that manufacture agility equipment. Enjoy!

Artist: Bud Houston

Agility Organizations

United States Dog Agility Association (USDAA)
P.O. Box 850995, Richardson, Texas 75085-0955;
Tel: 214-231-9700

American Kennel Club (AKC)
5580 Centerview Drive, Suite 200, Raleigh, NC 27606-3390;
Tel: 919-233-9767

North American Dog Agility Council (NADAC)
HCR 2, Box 277, St. Maries, Idaho 83861;
Tel: 208-689-3803

Australian Shepherd Club of America (ASCA)
6091 East State Highway 21, Bryan, Texas 77803-9652;
Tel: 409-778-1082

United Kennel Club (UKC)
100 East Kilgore Road, Kalamazoo, Michigan 49001-5593;
Tel: 616-343-9020

Agility Association of Canada (AAC)
638 Wonderland Road South, London, Ontario, N6K 1L8 Canada;
Tel: 519-473-3410

Agility Books

The Agility Dog International. Peter Lewis. Canine Publications, 21 Burridge Road, Burridge, Southampton SO3 7BY England; Tel: 0489 885112.

Agility is Fun! Books 1 & 2. Ruth Hobday. Our Dogs Publishing Company Ltd., 5 Oxford Road, Station Approach, Manchester M60 1SX England.

Agility Training for the Small Dog. (Book and video). Eva M. Martin. 2275 Huntington Drive #276, San Marino, CA 91108; 818-798-8110.

Agility Training: The Fun Sport for All Dogs. Jane Simmons-Moake. Howell Book House, Macmillan Publishing Company, 866 Third Avenue, New York, NY 10022.

The Clothier Natural Jumping Method. Suzanne Clothier. Contact: Flying Dog Press, PO Box 290, Stanton, NJ 08885; 1-800-7-FLY-DOG or 908-689-9426.

Enjoying Dog Agility. Julie Daniels. Doral Publishing, PO Box 596, Wilsonville, OR 97070.

Introductory Agility Workbook. Clean Run Productions, 35 Walnut Street, Turners Falls, MA 01376; 413-863-8303. Also available: *Intermediate Agility Workbook* and *Advanced Agility Workbook.*

Jumping from A to Z: Teaching Your Dog to Soar. M. Christine Zink D.V.M., Ph.D. and Julie Daniels. Canine Sports Productions, 1810A York Road #360, Lutherville, MD 21093; 410-561-1555.

Teaching Agility. Peter Lewis and John Gilbert. Canine Publications, 21 Burridge Road, Burridge, Southampton SO3 7BY England; Tel: 0489 885112.

Recommended Non-Agility Reading

Don't Shoot the Dog! Karen Pryor. Sunshine Books, 44811 S.E. 166th Street, N. Bend, WA 98045; 206-888-4708.

Peak Performance: Coaching the Canine Athlete. M. Christine Zink, D.V.M., Ph.D. Howell Book House, Macmillan Publishing Company, 866 Third Avenue, New York, NY 10022.

That Winning Feeling! Jane Savoie. Trafalgar Square Publishing. No. Pomfret, VT 05053. 800-423-4525.

Agility and Agility-Related Periodicals

Clean Run. Clean Run Productions, 35 Walnut Street, Turners Falls, MA 01376; 413-863-8303.

The Contact Line. Cascade Publications, 401 Bluemont Circle, Manhattan, KS 66502-4531.

Canine Sports Medicine Update. Geoffrey N. Clark D.V.M., PO Box 351, Newmarket, NH 03857.

Agility Videos

"Agility is Fun". Ruth Hobday. Available from Jean MacKenzie's Howling Moon Agility Stuff & More, 291 Ye Olde Canterbury Road, Northwood, NH 03261; 603-942-5717.

"Problems 1 & Problems 2". Ruth Hobday. Available from Jean MacKenzie's Howling Moon Agility Stuff & More.

"Control Exercises". Ruth Hobday. Available from Jean MacKenzie's Howling Moon Agility Stuff & More.

"Pups Progress". Ruth Hobday. Available from Jean MacKenzie's Howling Moon Agility Stuff & More.

"Introduction to Focus, Food & Fun". Patty Ruzzo. 334 Buckley Hill Road, Colchester, CT 06415.

"Your Athletic Dog: A Functional Approach". Suzanne Clothier (video and book). Flying Dog Press, PO Box 290, Stanton, NJ 08885; 1-800-7-FLY-DOG or 908-689-9426.

Agility Equipment

Action K-9 Sports Equipment by Amigos Enterprises. 27425 Cataluna Circle, Sun City, CA 92585; 909-679-3699.

EconoJumps. 1517 N. Wilmont Road, #111, Tucson, AZ; 520-751-1077.

Homestead Farm. 12 Chestnut Street, N. Brookfield, MA 01535; 508-867-5780.

On Course. P.O. Box 463, Branchville, NJ 07826; 800-942-5216.

Pipe Dreams by MAX200. 114 Beach Street, Rockaway, NJ 07866; 1-800-446-2920.

Paw Z Tracks. Box 39, Site 1, RR #7, Calgary, Alberta, T2P 2G7 Canada; 403-248-8744.

Artist: Jo Ann Mather

Training Methodology Q&A

Since the first printing of the *Introductory Agility Workbook* we have received a few requests for elaboration of the rationale behind some of the training methodologies described in this workbook.

- **Why are weave poles introduced in the first lesson?**

  The weave poles are the obstacle that requires the most repetition to learn. You will need all eight weeks of the program to give the dog a solid introduction to the poles. In addition, your students will never be more excited than they are on the first day of class. Introducing the weave poles on day one tends to leave a more positive impression in their minds; whereas putting off the introduction of the weave poles for a future session can add to the impression that many people have of them as a difficult and intimidating obstacle. Although the weave poles may take longer to learn than other obstacles, they can and should be fun!

- **Why is the dogwalk introduced before the A-frame?**

  While in a class situation it may seem like a better idea to teach the A-frame first because students want immediate gratification and it's relatively easy to scramble dogs up and over the wide ramps of the A-frame; There are, however, several reasons to introduce the dogwalk before the A-frame:

  1) It makes backchaining easier, especially if you are working with bigger dogs. You can easily position one or even two spotters on each side of the ramp and it's easier to get the dog positioned where you want him. It also forces the backchaining process to be slow—if you start backchaining on the A-frame, the dog is backed up to the ascent side almost immediately. The dogwalk is 36' long, which gives you plenty of time and space to solidify the concept in the dog's mind.

  2) The dogwalk makes the dog thoughtful of what his feet are doing while still at ground level. If you sit a dog on the end of the down ramp and entice him with food, he has to think about staying on the plank. If he steps off the side, there is no consequence (no danger) other than no food. But the dog is aware that the plank isn't there and will usually feel around and put his foot back up. (This is particularly useful for "wide-based" dogs as they learn at step 1 that they need to think about their feet and balancing.) Whereas, it is highly unlikely that even a dog that isn't being careful about placing his feet will step off the side of the A-frame ramp.

  3) Once you have backchained across the entire low dogwalk and have a reliable stop, you can *encourage* speed; and because of the length of the dogwalk, the dog can actually accelerate on the obstacle. Ideally, you should use a low, wide dogwalk (not a 9" plank) to encourage the dog to fly across as quickly as possible. Because the dog has learned to *race* across and put on the brakes at the end of the ramp, he has learned the beginnings of what's necessary for him to descend the A-frame ramp in a controlled manner. If the dog first learn contacts on a "short" obstacle like the A-frame, or on a very narrow dogwalk (9" wide), he never learns to "blast" across the obstacle.

  4) In the actual use of this program, dogs that learn the dogwalk *first* immediately take to the A-frame and transfer the pause in the contact and wait for release. It has not appeared that the opposite true.

  5) Dogs seem to have less dogwalk/teeter confusion when taught the dogwalk, then the A-frame, and then the teeter as opposed to the A-frame, then the dogwalk, and then the teeter. Maybe because once you have introduced the dogwalk and then you teach the A-frame, the dog comes to realize that all climbing obstacles are *not* the same; therefore they don't expect them all to be the same.